MARRIAGE MODELS

MARRIAGE MODELS

A Comprehensive Guide for Equipping Singles, Married, Divorced,
Marriage Counsellors, Pastors, and Parents.

TEMIDAYO ADEWOLE

XULON PRESS

Xulon Press
2301 Lucien Way #415
Maitland, FL 32751
407.339.4217
www.xulonpress.com

© 2021 by Temidayo Adewole

For inquiries and bulk distribution, please contact:
The Oracles of God
P.O. Box 25075,
Truro, NS
Canada
B2N 7B8
Email: oracles@rehobothsprings.ca

Unless otherwise indicated, Scripture quotations taken from the
King James Version (KJV) – *public domain.*

Paperback ISBN-13: 978-1-6628-0417-5

Ebook ISBN-13: 978-1-6628-0418-2

Dedication

This book is dedicated to:
God the Father who gave His only begotten Son;
Jesus Christ our Lord and Savior who gave His life a propitiation
for our sins;
The Holy Spirit, who continues to beckon on all men to come to
the knowledge of truth

Contents

Dedication v

Acknowledgment ix

Prologue xi

Disclaimer xv

Chapter One
Necessary Clarifications 1

Chapter Two
God's Will: What About It? 15

Chapter Three
Why Do Medical Test? 19

Marriage Models
What You Need To Know
About These Marriage Models 29

Chapter Four
Conservative Model. 31

Chapter Five
Assumption Model 37

Chapter Six
Independent Model. 41

Chapter Seven
Lacuna Model 45

Chapter Eight
Elusive Model 49

Chapter Nine
Traditional Model 53

Chapter Ten
Free Range Model 59

Chapter Eleven
Probability Model 63

Chapter Twelve
Genesis Model 67

Chapter Thirteen
Harmatia Model 71

Chapter Fourteen
Exceptional Rule Model. 75

Chapter Fifteen
Compassionate Model. 79

Chapter Sixteen
Marital Spindles 81

Chapter Seventeen
Important Clarifications For
The Married Seeking Divorce. 93

Template Of Courtship Conversations
For Intending Couples. 113

Endnotes 141

Acknowledgment

I thank Deborah, my wife, and burden-bearer, who has tirelessly, selflessly, and lovingly labored with me for the Lord in many places, and under several difficult circumstances. May the Lord reward the hours of sleep and comfort you invested and sacrificed while editing this book.

And to Daniel and 'Dara, thank you for your understanding and prayers all through the way.

Prologue

Marriage is one of the most critical and vital institutions that God established. Unfortunately, the devil has introduced so many deceptions into the world about marriage to confuse humanity. Many church folks are as confused as those in the world. While God seeks to settle the solitary in families, Satan, on the other hand, does work day and night to hinder the realization of God's beautiful and glorious plan. The devil does not want anyone to enjoy the honor that God reserves for marriage (Heb. 13:4).

In every generation, the arch-enemy of homes and marriages tries to hinder men and women from following the path that would lead them into successful marital experiences. I want to let you know that he is still very much around. Therefore, "Be sober, be vigilant; because your adversary the devil, as a roaring lion, walketh about, seeking whom he may devour" (1 Peter 5:8).

My interaction with Christians in many countries worldwide indicates that many churches have not provided or are not providing sufficient details to youths to guide them towards a successful relationship and purposeful marital journey. I also believe that several married couples and Christian leaders would need the information contained in this book.

A lot has been said and preached in Christianity, but very little has been put in place to answer the youth's quest in this generation. Many parents are not willing to talk about relationships, and several churches also feel it is probably not a very spiritual subject to engage with the youths.

Nevertheless, when satisfactory answers are not provided at home and in the church, it is natural for people to go elsewhere for the needed solutions. Unfortunately, the consequences of seeking solutions outside of Christ usually end in regret. As children grow, they must have a strong Christian perspective about relationships and marital issues. As the church grows, we cannot overemphasize the necessity to coordinate and regulate intentional relationships among the younger generations.

My primary motivation and the inspiration for writing this book is to give Christians a clear understanding of what marriage and relationship is all about.

In chapter one, I provided necessary clarifications on most of the questions that young Christians, married couples, and divorced individuals have asked or would love to ask.

Through the lens of Scriptures, chapter two explains what Christians need to know about "God's will" in marriage. It is crucial that you carefully go through this section as the phrase – "God's will" has become one of the most abused terminologies among Christians. Chapter three expounded on the Christian views about medical tests in a relationship intended to end in marriage. Besides the clarifications, I also provided illustrative charts to make the details easy to grasp for people with little or zero medical or science background. Many are wallowing in the pool of regrets today and wished they had known these realities before they got married to the person they fell in love with many years ago.

As you journey through chapters four to fifteen, you will come face-to-face with the realities of various marriage models that 'Christians' or 'churchgoers' practice. After considering all these models, you may wonder which of these models is the best. There is no need to be worried as chapter sixteen clarifies God's purpose for marriage. In addition to the merits and demerits under each model, I believe this section of the book would help you understand what God's perfect will is vis-à-vis the twelve different models. I saw the need to conclude with chapter seventeen, which focuses on biblical and necessary clarifications to Christians seeking a divorce. There are also appendices of courtship template discussions that intending couples might find useful.

From Adam to all the prophets and into the New Testament, God has always made clear, His perfect will to those who seek after Him. God is always willing to reveal His perfect will to each of His children in marriage. Every Christian needs to know this truth.

God made it easy for Adam:

And the Lord God caused a deep sleep to fall upon Adam, and he slept: and he took one of his ribs, and closed up the flesh instead thereof; and the rib, which the Lord God had taken from man, made he a woman, and brought her unto the man. And Adam said, This is now bone of my bones, and flesh of my flesh: she shall be called Woman, because she was taken out of Man." (Genesis 2:21-23).

Jeremiah told us, *"The word of the Lord came also unto me, saying, thou shalt not take thee a wife, neither shalt thou have sons or daughters in this place."* (Jeremiah 16:2).

Even a heathen King, named Abimelech in the Bible, was not left in the dark when he wanted to err on this matter. He was neither a follower of God nor a Bible-reader. However, God saw his innocence and showed him His perfect will. Unlike many Christians who jettisoned divine caution and beckoning before they got yoked unequally in marriage, the king of Gerar obeyed the Lord (Genesis 20:2-18). Abimelech II, who reigned during Isaac's era, must have read the story of his predecessor, Abimelech I, and he did not make a similar mistake (Gen. 26:8-10).

After many years of marriage, many people are regretting today. Several folks in the church today wished they had listened to such caution before they said, *"I DO."* Regrettably, it is too late to cry when the head is off.

Therefore, it seemed good to me, having had a perfect under-standing of all *these* things, to put this book together, as inspired by God. Please read and share with others before they make mistakes.

Understanding the panoramic overview of the merits and demerits of the different models of marriage practiced among individuals in churches and families today is a necessary tool for both the married and unmarried. It will aid your decision-making process. To a large extent, this book will show you the possible consequences that might trail your marital choices, even before you make those choices! The best way to forearm people is to fore-warn them. I believe this book will be a blessing to the body of Christ, globally.

Knowledge is power, and if you understand how these things work and make wise and godly decisions, your life and marriage would be sweet and blissful.

I welcome you on board to explore this complex and exciting book – MARRIAGE MODELS.

It is the first of its kind! The priceless wisdom and revelatory understanding it presents will enrich your Christian life.

Temidayo Adewole

Disclaimer

This book, in its entirety, is intended to provide general scriptural guidelines for Bible-believing Christians. None of the materials contained therein is intended to serve as and does not constitute recommendations or legal advice. Because marriage processes and issues are evolving and may vary among cultures, churches, and families, it could also involve legal implications. Therefore, the reader should consult medical, professional, or legal counsels for their marriages.

The author has coined the models' names based on their peculiarities and the people's experiences in the situations. Most of the merits and demerits were those submitted by people in those situations, while the remaining are the author's views based on his experience.

Where the names and scenarios used under any of the models resembles that of any person or organization, or there is any perceived slight of any individual or organization, it is purely coincidental.

While the author has produced this book's contents, he does not guarantee that the reader will experience all the merits or demerits highlighted under any of the models if they follow it. Your experience will depend on how you go about your marriage.

CHAPTER ONE

Necessary Clarifications

Why is it necessary for a man to leave his father and mother before getting joined to his wife?

The man is commanded to leave his parents for a reason. Marriage is God's brainchild, and He knows what will not make it work well. Your marriage may not work well if you abandon this foundational instruction. As a Christian, you must be intentional about enjoying and fulfilling God's purpose for your marriage. There are several purposes of marriage in the Scriptures, summarized into seven – procreation, purity, preservation, pleasure, perfection, protection, and productivity. Every couple needs a certain degree of freedom and liberty from their parents before these purposes can become a reality in their lives.

When is the right time to leave?

While there is no right age set in the Scriptures for this to happen, there are signs and signals that would indicate when the time is ripe. The Scriptures injuncts that children remain under the authority of their parents until marriage. While the man could leave when he becomes matured enough to establish his own family, the woman is required to remain under her parent's

authority until she is "given out" in marriage. Following her marriage, she would no longer remain under her father's authority.
The power over her head is transferred to her husband. Even if
she is living on her own prior to marriage, she is still considered
to be under her father's authority. The first question usually asked
in many churches on the wedding day is, **"who is giving this
woman in marriage?"** Although the man is to leave his parents,
the woman is to be given in marriage. This is a consistent pattern
in the Scriptures.

*Unto the woman he said, I will greatly multiply thy sorrow and thy
conception; in sorrow thou shalt bring forth children; and thy desire
shall be to thy husband, and he shall rule over thee* (Gen. 3:16).

*If a man vow a vow unto the Lord, or swear an oath to bind his soul
with a bond; he shall not break his word, he shall do according to all that
proceedeth out of his mouth. If a woman also vow a vow unto the Lord,
and bind herself by a bond, being in her father's house in her youth; and
her father hear her vow, and her bond wherewith she hath bound her
soul, and her father shall hold his peace at her; then all her vows shall
stand, and every bond wherewith she hath bound her soul shall stand.
But if her father disallow her in the day that he heareth; not any of her
vows, or of her bonds wherewith she hath bound her soul, shall stand:
and the Lord shall forgive her, because her father disallowed her. And
if she had at all an husband, when she vowed, or uttered ought out of
her lips, wherewith she bound her soul; and her husband heard it, and
held his peace at her in the day that he heard it: then her vows shall
stand, and her bonds wherewith she bound her soul shall stand. But if
her husband disallowed her on the day that he heard it; then he shall
make her vow which she vowed, and that which she uttered with her lips,
wherewith she bound her soul, of none effect: and the Lord shall forgive
her. But every vow of a widow, and of her that is divorced, wherewith
they have bound their souls, shall stand against her. And if she vowed
in her husband's house, or bound her soul by a bond with an oath; And
her husband heard it, and held his peace at her, and disallowed her not:
then all her vows shall stand, and every bond wherewith she bound her*

soul shall stand. But if her husband hath utterly made them void on the day he heard them; then whatsoever proceeded out of her lips concerning her vows, or concerning the bond of her soul, shall not stand: her husband hath made them void; and the Lord shall forgive her. Every vow, and every binding oath to afflict the soul, her husband may establish it, or her husband may make it void. But if her husband altogether hold his peace at her from day to day; then he establisheth all her vows, or all her bonds, which are upon her: he confirmeth them, because he held his peace at her in the day that he heard them. But if he shall any ways make them void after that he hath heard them; then he shall bear her iniquity. These are the statutes, which the Lord commanded Moses, between a man and his wife, between the father and his daughter, being yet in her youth in her father's house (Num. 30:1-16).

But if any man think that he behaveth himself uncomely toward his virgin, if she pass the flower of her age, and need so require, let him do what he will, he sinneth not: let them marry. Nevertheless he that standeth stedfast in his heart, having no necessity, but hath power over his own will, and hath so decreed in his heart that he will keep his virgin, doeth well. So then he that giveth her in marriage doeth well; but he that giveth her not in marriage doeth better. The wife is bound by the law as long as her husband liveth; but if her husband be dead, she is at liberty to be married to whom she will; only in the Lord (1 Cor. 7:36-39).

Under what circumstances would 'leaving' be wrong?

As noted above, it would be contrary to the Scriptures for a man or a woman to leave their parents and start living together without their parents' consent, particularly the woman (1 Cor. 7:36-38).

"If her father utterly refuses to give her unto him, he shall pay money according to the dowry of virgins" (Exo. 22:17).

Some have argued that Isaac and Jacob's marriages were elopements (i.e., without parents' consent). Such reasoning is not right. In the cases of Isaac and Jacob, both parents gave their permission and blessings.

3

In the case of Isaac, Abraham gave his consent. See Abraham's consent below:

And Abraham said unto his eldest servant of his house, that ruled over all that he had, Put, I pray thee, thy hand under my thigh: and I will make thee swear by the Lord, the God of heaven, and the God of the earth, that thou shalt not take a wife unto my son of the daughters of the Canaanites, among whom I dwell: but thou shalt go unto my country, and to my kindred, and take a wife unto my son Isaac (Gen. 24:2-4).

As for Rebekah, Bethuel also gave his consent and prayers:

Then Laban and Bethuel answered and said, the thing proceedeth from the LORD: we cannot speak unto thee bad or good. Behold, Rebekah is before thee, take her, and go, and let her be thy master's son's wife, as the LORD hath spoken. And it came to pass, that, when Abraham's servant heard their words, he worshipped the LORD, bowing himself to the earth. And the servant brought forth jewels of silver, and jewels of gold, and raiment, and gave them to Rebekah: he gave also to her brother and to her mother precious things. And they did eat and drink, he and the men that were with him, and tarried all night; and they rose up in the morning, and he said, Send me away unto my master. And her brother and her mother said, Let the damsel abide with us a few days, at the least ten; after that she shall go. And he said unto them, Hinder me not, seeing the LORD hath prospered my way; send me away that I may go to my master. And they said, We will call the damsel, and enquire at her mouth. And they called Rebekah, and said unto her, Wilt thou go with this man? And she said, I will go. And they sent away Rebekah their sister, and her nurse, and Abraham's servant, and his men. And they blessed Rebekah, and said unto her, Thou art our sister, be thou the mother of thousands of millions, and let thy seed possess the gate of those which hate them (Gen. 24:50-60).

In the case of Jacob, Isaac gave his consent:

And Isaac called Jacob, and blessed him, and charged him, and said unto him, Thou shalt not take a wife of the daughters of Canaan. Arise, go to Padanaram, to the house of Bethuel thy mother's father; and take thee a wife from thence of the daughters of Laban thy mother's brother. And God Almighty bless thee, and make thee fruitful, and multiply thee, that thou mayest be a multitude of people; and give thee the blessing of Abraham, to thee, and to thy seed with thee; that thou mayest inherit the land wherein thou art a stranger, which God gave unto Abraham. And Isaac sent away Jacob: and he went to Padanaram unto Laban, son of Bethuel the Syrian, the brother of Rebekah, Jacob's and Esau's mother (Gen. 28:1-5).

And Laban also gave his consent in both cases for Racheal and Leah.

And Laban gathered together all the men of the place, and made a feast. And it came to pass in the evening, that he took Leah his daughter, and brought her to him; and he went in unto her. And Laban gave unto his daughter Leah Zilpah his maid for an handmaid. And Laban said, It must not be so done in our country, to give the younger before the firstborn. Fulfil her week, and we will give thee this also for the service which thou shalt serve with me yet seven other years. And Jacob did so, and fulfilled her week: and he gave him Rachel his daughter to wife also. And Laban gave to Rachel his daughter Bilhah his handmaid to be her maid (Gen. 29: 22-24; 26-29).

What is cleaving, and what does it entail?

Cleaving refers to the joining of both the man and his wife in a life-long covenant. It entails an exclusive bonding between a man and his wife to become one unit before God. This oneness denotes independence and uniqueness. God expects each family to run as a nuclear unit, free from all forms of external interferences that could wreck it. Parents and relatives must respect this divine instruction. Nevertheless, the union of married couples does not preclude them from interacting with their relations and siblings. There could be situations that may warrant a married couple to stay temporarily with their relatives and vice-versa.

Nevertheless, it is not God's idea that everything going on in your marriage be broadcasted to third parties or posted for public consumption on social media. Somebody must mature before embarking on the marriage journey as it requires every sense of maturity, without which the marriage may not succeed. That is one reason why marriage as an institution must be consummated by a man and a woman, not a boy and a girl.

As established in the Scriptures, God expects marital oneness to reflect in every area of a couple's life. Marriage requires spiritual, emotional, physical, moral, financial, and sexual commitments.

What? Know ye not that he who is joined to a harlot is one body with her? "For two," saith He, "shall be one flesh (1 Cor. 6:16).

However, the unity between couples must breed a mutually desired result in the same way the product of a sexual union produces a child that carries the genetic information from both parents.

You may have your differences, yet you must disagree to agree. To be united only in sex and divided in every other way is neither God's way nor His will.

Can two walk together, except they be agreed? (Amos 3:3).

When is cleaving not acceptable to God?

God instituted marriage, and He alone is the principal witness (Mal. 2:14). Even though the world's culture and systems may change as new laws evolve across different countries, God's standard in His word remains valid. According to the Scriptures, any cleaving that fall within any of the following categories is not approved of God:

i. **Cleaving to a divorcee**

It hath been said, whosoever shall put away his wife, let him give her a writing of divorcement: but I say unto you, That whosoever shall put away his wife, saving for the cause of fornication, causeth her to commit adultery: and whosoever shall marry her that is divorced committeth adultery (Matt. 5:31,32).

ii. **Cleaving without fulfilling the requirements of her parents**

If her father utterly refuse to give her unto him, he shall pay money according to the dowry of virgins (Exo. 22:17;).

iii. **Cleaving between same-genders**

Thou shalt not lie with mankind, as with womankind: it is abomination (Lev. 18:22; Rom. 1:26-32; 1 Cor. 6:9).

iv. **Cleaving to someone whose spouse is still alive**

For the woman which hath an husband is bound by the law to her husband so long as he liveth; but if the husband be dead, she is loosed from the law of her husband. So then if, while her husband liveth, she be married to another man, she shall be called an adulteress: but if her husband be dead, she is free from that law; so that she is no adulteress, though she be married to another man (Romans 7:2, 3; 1 Cor. 7:39).

v. **Cleaving to animals**

Neither shalt thou lie with any beast to defile thyself therewith: neither shall any woman stand before a beast to lie down thereto: it is confusion (Leviticus 18:23).

vi. **Cleaving to close relative**

None of you shall approach to any that is near of kin to him, to uncover their nakedness: I am the Lord (Lev. 18:6).

vii. **Cleaving to more than one spouse at the same time (Bigamy or Polygamy)**

Therefore shall a man leave his father and his mother, and shall cleave unto his wife: and they shall be one flesh (Gen. 2:24).

How can young folks today manage the challenges of "time" and "timing" regarding leaving and cleaving?

The period of singleness has a lot of merits. It is the best time to begin to access the mind of God concerning your purpose in life. God designed this period of freedom to be used wisely to build a good foundation for the future. Failure to maximize this period could be a foundation for subsequent failures in the future. It takes two people who have been successful as singles to have a successful marriage. This stage of singleness in your life is the bedrock for your marriage. It is the foundation. If the foundation is faulty, the marriage may not work well. During this window of opportunity, God wants you to develop a profound depth of fellowship with Him. Undeniably, this season could also breed loneliness, emotional struggles, and a search for identity in the context of a complex society. The way you use this period would either mar or make your marriage in the years ahead. My candid counsel for young people is that they use this period for character, spiritual, professional, and personal development. When the time for marriage comes, they will be ready and fit for it.

Can you leave after cleaving?

There is no God-approved provision for leaving after you have cleaved in marriage. Marriage is a covenant that is valid until one of the parties dies. If you are duly married to each other, your marriage is valid in God's eyes till death. Even if you separate and start living apart, God still sees you as being married to each other. I have provided more clarifications in chapter seventeen of this book.

What therefore God hath joined together, let not man put asunder (Mark 10:9).

When does "leaving and cleaving" become irrational?

These are the various categories of abnormalities that have now become commonplace everywhere today.

- **Married but living separately:** These are couples who got married but are living separately for very long periods. This is a growing trend both within and outside the church. Sometimes it is due to career pursuit or some family ties. In any of these cases, it is crucial to understand that God's perfect will for couples who have been appropriately joined in holy matrimony is to live together under the same roof. Whatever separates couples for a long time, at the expense of the union's divine and constructive purposes, contradicts the perfect will of God.
- **Living with parents or being tied to parents after marriage for a long time:** If you are married, it is an aberration for you to be more bonded to your parents than your spouse. If a tie to your parents is hindering your cleaving to your spouse, it may be needful that you go for spiritual help. Both history and experiences have often shown that such causes of marital separations are offshoots of satanic activities operational against the couple's lives. The enemy could use anything to separate couples so that they would never come to the realization and fulfillment of God's plan for their marriage. There could also be covenants that must be broken if you are closer to your parents/siblings than your spouse and children. I knew a couple who got married, but the husband's family diabolically tied him to the city where he was born. The wife worked in another state in a federal establishment while the husband worked in his hometown in an organization where his income could barely meet his personal needs.

After much prayers by his wife, God provided a lucrative job opportunity in an organization that could bring him to the same location where his wife worked and lived with their kids. Unfortunately, his siblings advised him to remain with them in their hometown. He did not take the job offer! That was a spiritual tie! He continued shuttling between his wife's location and his hometown for several years. The wife could not understand why. After several years, he decided to relocate to join his wife and children. The same month he relocated, one of his siblings called him to come to their hometown. He left but never to return! A family member later confessed that the accident that claimed his life was diabolically arranged.

If you are noticing any of these patterns in your life or in someone you know, it will be advisable to seek spiritual help from a spiritually sound minister of the gospel. You might need to go for counseling and pray against the yoke of family ties before it gets too late. Many people have shared testimonies of how they were delivered from similar yokes through the power of Jesus' name.

Shall the prey be taken from the mighty, or the lawful captive delivered? But thus saith the Lord, Even the captives of the mighty shall be taken away, and the prey of the terrible shall be delivered: for I will contend with him that contendeth with thee, and I will save thy children (Ish. 49:24-25).

If you are a Christian and you are not living with your spouse and children in the name of ministry or church work, you need to reconsider your situation prayerfully. God cannot put asunder what He has graciously joined since He is not the author of confusion. Any ministry, career pursuit, or business attainment that discountenanced your marital union perpetually may not be the perfect will of God. It is often either your own will, the manipulation of men, or the enemy's handiwork.

- **Those who believe their marriage was a mistake**
  I have had conversations with some men who told me
  their marriages to their wives were mistakes! In an
  attempt to remarry, one said, "God winked at the times
  of *his* ignorance" (Acts 17:30-31). I told him he had mis-
  applied that Scripture. God cannot contradict Himself.
  You cannot divorce (disobey the word of God) to do God's
  will. That is one reason why it is imperative to take every
  caution before entering into the marriage covenant. In
  the beginning, God instituted marriage to be a relationship between a man and a woman (Matt. 19:4,5). Hence,
  God is the primary witness in every marriage relationship,
  conducted per His pattern — whether they are believers or
  non-believers.
  According to the Scriptures, every lawful marriage remains
  valid until death do them part. While it is true that God's
  word admonishes believers to marry in the Lord (2 Cor.
  6:14,15), if a believer enters into a marriage covenant with
  an unbeliever, he or she is bound by the covenant (Mal.
  2:14; 1 Cor. 7:12).

Another man who wanted to divorce his wife once asked this
question — **"was marriage made for man or man was made for
marriage?"**
I understood that this was a logical question as the questioner
tried to equate marriage with Sabbath. See my response to this
question below:
**"God made the sabbath for man. Man was not made for
the sabbath.** Sabbath was made for all men; however, they are
not bound by it. What is important to God is for man is to have
a day to rest and worship Him. **God gives man the privilege to
do what is good and best for himself on his days of rest** (Matt.
12:8; Mark 2:27-28; 3:4; Luke 6:9).

On the other hand, marriage was not made for all men, for some are not made to marry (Matt. 19:10-12). However, anyone that chooses to marry brings himself under the marriage covenant, and he or she is bound by it (Rom. 7:2).

In the context of the question, **God made marriage for man, but unlike the sabbath, God did not give man the privilege to do whatever he feels good for himself while his or her spouse lives** (Matt. 19:6; Mark 10:9). According to the Scriptures, God says He is the main witness to the marriage covenant. That is why He said, **let not man** put asunder. The phrase—**let not man** means no human being (including the couple, judge, parents, or any other person) has the authority to dissolve a marriage that God serves as witness. Jesus corrected the notion of divorce in Matthew 19:6-9. Death is the only thing that God permits to end the marriage covenant (Rom. 7:2; 1 Cor. 7:39). Now, a question that may readily come to mind is: Can someone pray to God for his or her spouse to die? **The answer is NO.** God cannot be tempted with such an evil thought or act (James 1:13)."

Another question was asked, **"In a covenant, when a party breaks the terms of the covenant, is the covenant still valid?"** See my response below:

It depends on the type of covenant and the conditions attached to the covenant. Covenant can be between humans or between God and man. In either case, both parties are bound by whatsoever conditions that they agreed upon. In most general covenants between men, the parties involved can agree on certain things as conditions binding them together (Gen. 21:22-34; 26:26-33; 1 Sam. 18:3,4). If they agreed that breaking the condition ends the contract, the faithful person may opt-out if the other fails to keep the terms of their agreement. However, covenants between people may become more difficult to break if it involves a "deity or a god." That's why certain ancestral issues are very problematic.

For example, the Israelites could not come out of the covenant they unwittingly entered into with the Gibeonites (Josh.

9:14-19) because they made the covenant in the name of the God of Israel. Hence they could not just come out of it. Hundreds of years later, King Saul broke the covenant without prayers or offering any sacrifice, and a severe famine came upon the entire nation of Israel. When David inquired from God, God told him, *It is for Saul, and for his bloody a house, because he slew the Gibeonites* (2 Sam. 21:2). David prayed, but God did not answer because He is a covenant-keeping God. Until the demand of that covenant was granted, there was no peace in Israel (2 Sam. 21:1-14). Notably, the fact that the Gibeonites deceived the Israelites was no justification for the Jews to do whatever they liked to the Gibeonites. There might be severe consequences for anyone to break a covenant that involves any deity or a god. Anyone who wants to break such covenants must involve a power and authority superior to that of the deity/god who established the covenant. For this reason, only Jesus' name (which God has exalted above every other name) can deliver anyone under an ancestral / family covenants.

The second kind of covenant is the **God-Man Covenant**. In all covenants between God and man, God sets the conditions. Remarkably, the marriage covenant is not only an agreement between two people. It is essentially an agreement between two humans before God, and God puts Himself as a third party in the covenant (Mal. 2:14). In this case, God is the one who also established the condition binding the two humans in the covenant— **until death."**

The questioner further asked, **"Can God speak to someone about his or her marriage outside the Bible?"**

I answered, yes. God can speak to anyone using any means He feels will make His message clear to the person (Num. 22:28; Jer. 18:1-10). However, God will not speak to contradict Himself or His written word (1 Cor. 14:33). God already said He hates divorce (Mal. 2:16). Based on God's moral principles and His regard for His words (Num. 23:19; Tit. 1:2; Heb. 6:18), I believe He cannot and will not speak otherwise to any man (Mal. 3:6).

CHAPTER TWO

God's Will: What About It?

A lot has been said and taught about knowing God's will in marriage. Nevertheless, many Christians are still not clear about it. I trust God to use this little light to further illuminate your heart and mind on this subject of eternal importance. There could be imminent dangers if you do not get this right.

Who is God's will for you in marriage?

God's will for you in marriage is that person that God has prepared to meet the need of your life in marriage. Every marriageable man is created to need a woman to help him fulfill his purpose in life. However, you must understand that not every woman can fit into this role in your life. It is not even every Christian lady that can be your helpmeet. You need to seek God's face for who this particular person is.

The first thing I would like the men to appreciate is this — it is God's duty to prepare the woman for you. Therefore, the first step towards becoming a marriageable woman is to submit yourself for preparation in God's hands.

Christians seeking God's will in marriage must entrust their lives into God's hands and believe that He will surely bring His perfect choice into their lives at the right time. You might live to regret it if you arrange any spouse for yourself, without God's guidance.

When a man who has entrusted his life into God's hand meets the woman that God has prepared for him, he can never miss it. God will make the confirmation easy.

From the ideal marriage between Adam and Eve before the fall of humanity, the following are noteworthy:

- The man was already formed by God – *meaning maturity, stability, profitable engagement, and ability.*
- The man slept in God's arms – *denoting absolute trust in God*
- God prepared the woman from the rib taken out of the man – *indicating that God knew the deficiencies in a man's life, and He alone could prepare someone to meet the need in the life of every marriageable man.*
- God brought the woman to the man when he was awake – *implying that God is committed to bring the woman at the right time, when it will be easy for him to recognize her. Notice that it was not the woman that came to wake him up.*
- The man accepted the woman that God brought to him with joy and excitement – *symbolizing marital satisfaction.*

As simple as these instructions are, if you fail to understand these things, you may never realize what God has in store for you in marriage.

Is God's will limited to a particular person? I have known God's will, but he or she said no, what should I do? If I see someone as God's will, but the person sees another person as God's will, what should I do?

Every child of God is a potential will of God for another child of God. If the person that God has prepared for you refused to marry you or something happened (beyond your control), and you could not marry that person, God would prepare another person to meet your need. The person can change, but God's plan to give you an expected end will not change as long as you are faithful to him.

How do I know God's perfect will in marriage?

There is no particular method of knowing God's will in marriage. If everything is normal, children should know the voice of their father. God communicates with every Christian through various means, and we understand Him through the help of the Holy Spirit.

But as it is written, Eye hath not seen, nor ear heard, neither have entered into the heart of man, the things which God hath prepared for them that love him. But God hath revealed them unto us by his Spirit: for the Spirit searcheth all things, yea, the deep things of God. For what man knoweth the things of a man, save the spirit of man which is in him? even so the things of God knoweth no man, but the Spirit of God. Now we have received, not the spirit of the world, but the spirit which is of God; that we might know the things that are freely given to us of God (1 Cor. 2:9-12).

If you are a child of God, you must understand how God speaks to you. Jesus said, "my sheep hear my voice, and I know them, and they follow me" (John 10:27). Without clarity from God, you are likely to miss God's will and take a "bone and flesh" that belongs to someone else (Jer. 10:23; Prov. 16:9; 14:12).

In the past, I have met Christians who testified that God led them through various means such as confirmatory word of knowledge from God's servants, agape love, dreams, visions, divine revelations, inward impressions, spirit confirmation, scriptural principles, etc. These and many more are consistent with the word of God. Joseph was guided through dreams (Matt. 1:20); Jeremiah was guided through God's word (Jer. 16:2); Saul got a confirmatory word of knowledge from God's servants (1 Sam. 10:1-9, 16); Cornelius was led to Peter through a vision (Acts 10:1-6); Peter had a trance or vision (Acts 10: 19-21); Ananias also was guided through a vision (Acts 9:10-17), Paul had abundance of revelations (2 Cor. 12:7); Elizabeth had a spirit confirmation the moment she heard Mary's voice (Luke 1:41-45). God can use any means to lead and guide you. However, it is instructive that you pay attention to how God has been leading you on every other life issues to receive guidance when it comes to your marriage.

What should I look for in a potential marriage partner?

I have categorized what you might want to be sure to look out for in a potential marriage partner before you are wedded to three essential things:

1. **Christo-type** confirmation — This means he or she must be a type of Christ. In order words, a little Christ. Christo-type consideration covers everything you would love to see in Christ — spiritual attributes, secular responsibilities, professional advancements, and social disposition (Luke 2:52).
2. **Geno-type** compatibility — This refers to his or her genetic configuration. See chapter three for further details on this. You should consult your medical professional for advice on this aspect (1 John 4:1).
3. **Pheno-type** characteristics — This refers to the physical attributes of the person. You may not fall in love immediately when God reveals His perfect will to you. However, God must perfect your love for him or her before you tie the knot. Do not marry anyone out of sympathy. God will guide you, but He will never force or impose anyone on you (SOS 2:16; 6:3).

CHAPTER THREE

Why Do Medical Test?

Before marriage, it might be helpful to consider doing some medical tests such as a genotype test as soon as possible, preferably before you go too far in an intentional relationship. Suppose you wait until after you have gone too far in your relationship before checking your medical status and compatibility; any of the following could happen if you find out that you are not medically compatible.

- You may end up getting married out of sympathy and succumb to a lifelong regret as you may have to endure rather than enjoy your marital life.
- You might get married and watch one or more of your kids go through life in pain and anguish or eventually die.
- You may opt to end the relationship with heartaches because you are already in love with each other.
- You might as well encounter no challenge in the marriage.

GENOTYPE TEST
WHY DO GENOTYPE TEST?

Your genotype refers to your genetic make-up. Your genotype is the combination of the types of genes present in your blood as an individual. Each human being has two kinds of hemoglobin (Hb) genes in their blood. The only way you can get these genes is from your parents at birth. You can only get one hemoglobin gene from each parent. That is, one from your father and one from your mother. Therefore, the types of genes you inherited from your parents depends on the types of genes that your parents carry.

WHAT ARE THESE HEMOGLOBINS?

Recall that hemoglobin is the component of blood responsible for the transportation of oxygen in the body. Any abnormality of the hemoglobin could result in serious health issues and even death.

The typical and healthy hemoglobin gene is Hemoglobin A (HbA). All normal hemoglobin in the blood is round. The disklike shape of the hemoglobin makes it easy for it to travel within the blood vessels. There are several abnormal Hemoglobin genes.

For this book, the hemoglobin abnormality that causes the disease called **"Sickle cell anemia (HbS)** will be my focus.

WHAT IS ANEMIA?

Anemia means a shortage of normal healthy red blood cells in the body. Hemoglobin is part of the composition of every normal red blood cell. It is the part of the blood responsible for transporting oxygen from the lungs to all body tissues. Hence, reduced levels of hemoglobin will reduce the amount of oxygenated blood available to the body. Without an adequate supply of oxygen to vital parts of the body, death is imminent.

WHAT IS SICKLE CELL ANEMIA?

In sickle-cell anemia syndrome, the Hemoglobin cell S (HbS) structure is sickle-shaped instead of the typical round shapes of red blood cells.

HOW DOES THIS BECOME A PROBLEM?

The distorted or sickle-shaped cells cannot move freely through the blood vessels. Sickle-shaped cells may get stuck within the blood vessels, causing severe pain and decreased blood flow in the body. When this happens, reduced oxygen delivery to vital organs results, and the red cell cannot survive for too long.

WHAT ARE YOUR CHANCES?

The types of genotypes in most individuals includes but not limited to:
HbAA: Normal individual
HbAS: Sickle cell carrier
HbSS: Sickle-cell individual
If either you have a sickle cell trait (HbAS) and your partner does not carry the sickle hemoglobin at all (HbAA), none of the children will have sickle cell anemia.
Suppose you both have sickle cell traits in your blood. In that case, there is a possibility that one or more of your children might inherit the sickle cell hemoglobin gene either with a carrier-status or with the actual sickle cell anemia disease-status[1].

MARRIAGE MODELS

See the diagrams below for possible outcomes.

CHART 1

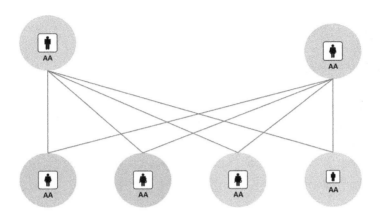

Fig. 1: Marriage between persons with genotypic combinations HbAA and HbAA
Probability of having a sickle cell anemic child is 0

CHART 2

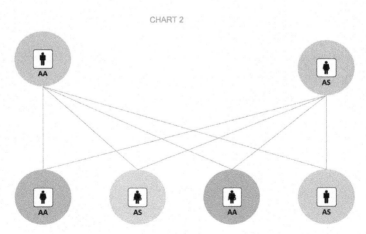

Fig. 2: Marriage between persons with genotypic combinations **HbAA** and **HbAS**
Probability of having a sickle cell anemic child from every conception is **0**

WHY DO MEDICAL TEST?

CHART 3

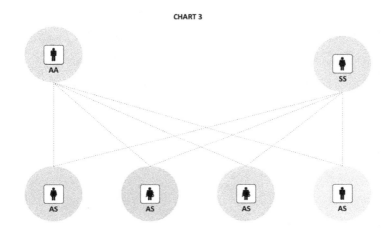

Fig. 3: Marriage between persons with genotypic combinations **HbAA** and **HbSS**

Probability of having a sickle cell anemic child from every conception is **0**

CHART 4

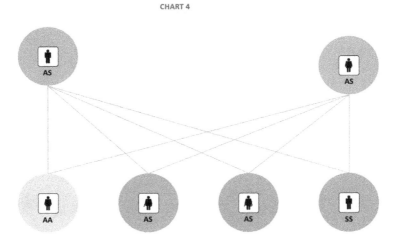

Fig. 4: Marriage between persons with genotypic combinations **HbAS** and **HbAS**

Probability of having a sickle cell anemic child in every conception is 0.25

MARRIAGE MODELS

CHART 5

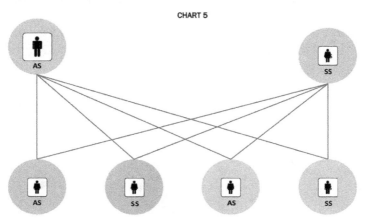

Fig. 5: Marriage between persons with genotypic combinations **HbAS** and **HbSS**

Probability of having a sickle cell anemic child from every conception is **0.5**

CHART 6

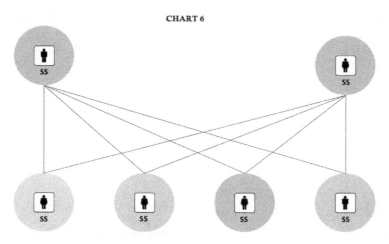

Fig. 6: Marriage between persons with genotypic combinations **HbSS** and **HbSS**

Probability of having a sickle cell anemic child from every conception is 1

BLOOD GROUP-RHESUS (RH) FACTOR

Generally, there are four types of blood – O, A, B, and AB. Each of these blood types could have either Rh positive or negative and may have any of the following blood types: O^{Rh+}, A^{Rh+}, B^{Rh+}, AB^{Rh+}, O^{Rh-}, A^{Rh-}, B^{Rh-}, and AB^{Rh-2}. Rhesus factors are proteins present in the red blood cells. Both blood types and Rh factors are genetically inherited from parents.

WHY DO A BLOOD GROUP RH FACTOR TEST?

If you are Rh-positive, you can receive a blood transfusion from people with Rh-negative. However, if your Rh factor is negative, it is medically dangerous to receive blood transfusion from a person with Rh-positive[2].

You should know the Rh Factor in your blood to avoid plunging your family into avoidable jeopardy after marriage. Knowing your status ahead of time may become critical to both your life and that of your babies. You should consult your physician for medical advice before it is too late.

WHAT IS THE DANGER?

During pregnancy, a woman with Rh-negative carrying a baby with Rh-positive blood may be advised to receive an injection of Rho (D) Immune Globulin to save future babies' lives or prevent future episodes of hemolytic disease of the newborn in her subsequent pregnancies.

You should consult your physician for medical advice. Several women had experienced one or more miscarriages before they knew that was the cause. Consult your physician for medical advice before it is too late.

See the summary of the above explanations below[3].

Blood Type	Can Give	Can Receive
A+	A+ and AB+	A+, A-, O+, and O-
O+	O+, A+, B+ and AB+	O+ and O-
B+	B+ and AB+	B+, B-, O+ and O-
AB+	AB+	All blood types
A-	A+, A-, AB+ and AB-	A- and O-
O-	All blood types	O-
B-	B+, B-, AB+ and AB-	B- and O-
AB-	AB+ and AB-	AB-, A, B- and O-

Table 1: Rhesus Factor Blood Donation Chart

OTHER IMPORTANT MEDICAL TESTS

VDRL TEST – This test may help to rule out latent or untreated syphilis, which may result in:

- brain, heart, bones, and nervous system damages in the future;
- infertility; and
- medical complications in the newborn, such as stillbirths and miscarriages.

VERIFY ANY MEDICAL IMPACT OF PREVIOUS SURGERIES DONE

There are have been stories of people who had surgeries that were not considered a problem before being married. However, after marriage, they could not have children of their own. You should get the medical history of your partner. Get professional advice from a qualified medical practitioner on any concerns you might have before getting married.

HUMAN IMMUNODEFICIENCY VIRUS 1 AND 2 (HIV-1/2) SCREENING

You might be skeptical about this. However, many married couples have found this to be helpful. Since there are several other ways of contracting the disease, you might want to consider this before the start of courtship and after the courtship before marriage to be sure you are safe. Marriage is a serious institution. You should be aware that you are about to make a lifetime decision. Prevention is better and cheaper than the cost of cure and repair.

HEPATITIS C TEST

Hepatitis C virus infects the liver, and the impacts could be grave. You should be aware of the medical implications of the person you wish to marry. There should be transparency in marriage. Hence, no medical information should be too sacred to share, especially if it could impact the life of your intending spouse and children. You and your proposed spouse need this information to decide if you would be comfortable moving ahead with the relationship or not. A broken courtship is far better than a broken and battered marriage. You should consult a qualified medical practitioner before it is too late.

MARRIAGE MODELS

What You Need To Know
About These Marriage Models

This section presents a panoramic overview of how Christians go about their marriages, based on their personal, cultural, family, and denominational preferences.

I have invented unique names for each model, based on the peculiarities and experiences of those involved in each model's scenarios.

Enjoy the narratives.

CHAPTER FOUR

Conservative Model

The conservative model is adopted by some churches, which believed that ladies were more prone to making mistakes or getting confused if numerous men make proposals to them at the same time. Hence, measures were put in place to regulate how men made proposals to them. Age was also an essential consideration under this model. Intending couples were not allowed to visit each other at home before marriage. However, the man's house was inspected by the Marriage Counselling unit of their church. As a result of the complexity of the conservative model, several other models emanated from it. Examples are exceptional rule, hamartia, and compassionate models.

SCENARIO ONE

Four men in the same fellowship/congregation felt God was leading them to marry a lady. All four were born-again. Each person believed he was sent by God to marry her!

SCENARIO TWO

Peter had been praying for the will of God in marriage since his undergraduate years. After graduation, he got a job as a lecturer at a university. Six months later, Bola also began work in the same university. The first day, Peter saw Bola, and the Holy Spirit confirmed in his heart that Bola would be his wife. Although they later attended the same church, Peter did not tell Bola anything about his leading towards her. He kept praying about it and believed God that "he that believeth should not make haste" (Isa. 28:16). That was the Scripture that has guided him on many other issues of life. After one year, he told his pastor about it. The pastor told him to approach the Marriage Counselling unit of the church (MCU). The MCU interviewed Peter and asked him to do specific medical tests.

Meanwhile, the MCU contacted Bola and asked her if she was praying for marriage. She told them yes. They also asked her to do specific medical tests. The MCU did not disclose to her the identity of the man who had shown interest in her. After several weeks of waiting, both results came out and with satisfactory genotypic compatibility. Peter was permitted to propose to Bola. He did, and Bola accepted. However, that was just the beginning. Peter reverted the outcome of his proposal to the MCU, and they were both invited for a tete-a-tete. Peter and Bola were instructed to inform their parents and get their consent about their intentions to marry each other, and both parents consented. They courted for eighteen months under the supervision of the MCU. At the end of their courtship, the MCU asked them to do another round of medical tests. The results were all good. Peter paid the dowry (as required in their culture). Afterward, they filed a notice with the court under the marriage constitution of their country. They did both traditional and church marriage. They are happily married with children.

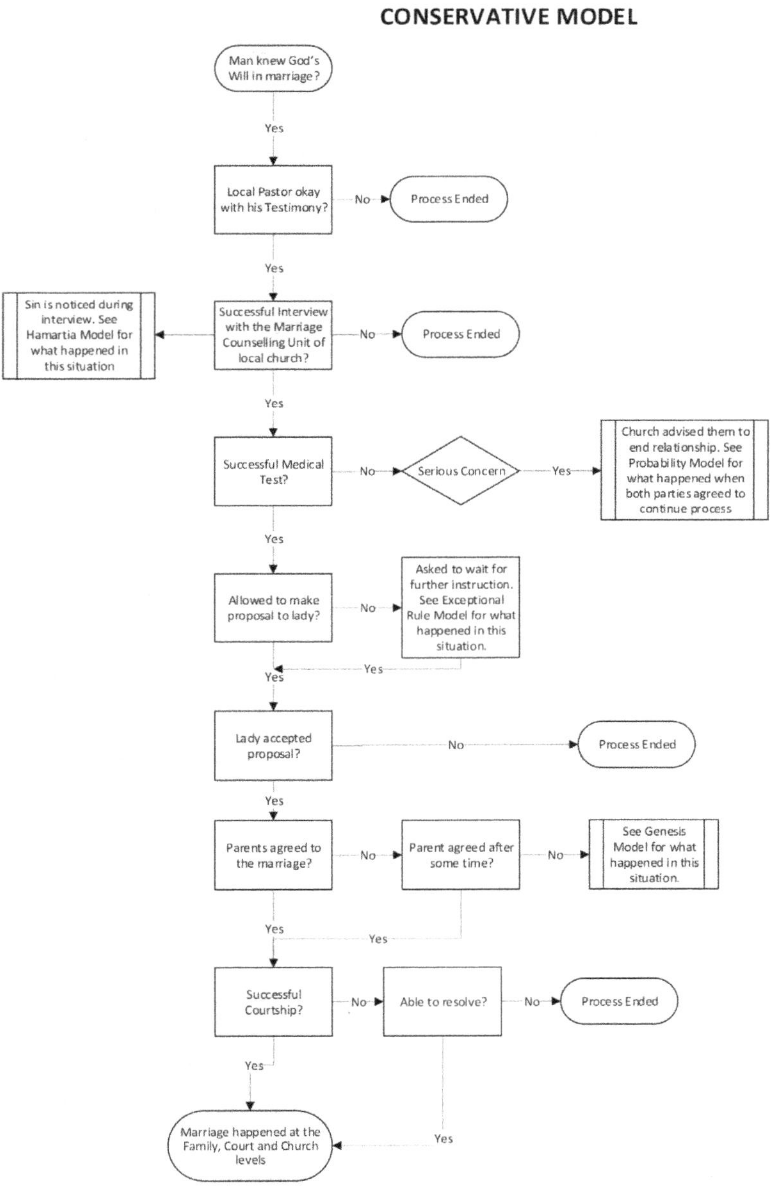

Fig 7: Conservative Model Chart

MERITS OF CONSERVATIVE MODEL

1. This model helped members to be more matured before making marital decisions.
2. It prevented deceivers from taking advantage of the innocent ones.
3. It helped intending partners to mediate difficult issues that they were not able to resolve between themselves.
4. It reduced the chances of being overtaken by immoral sin.
5. It helped relationships among brethren as things are done decently and in order.
6. It gave single ladies sufficient room to pray and seek counsel before accepting a marriage proposal.
7. There was enough time to seek to determine if it was God's perfect will for them to marry each other, and commitment to God and each other preceded intimacy.
8. There were opportunities to develop a friendship that could lead to marriage as they determined their marriage readiness under the protection, guidance, and blessing of parents and mentors.
9. Since no Christian could introduce two different individuals to their parents as a proposed marriage partner, it hindered anyone from playing games or simultaneously courting two different people.
10. The structured courtship arrangements helped intending partners to confirm or cancel their decisions.
11. It encouraged and promoted accountability to both parents and church leadership.
12. It promoted transparency among the church members.
13. It helps intending partners know themselves more before getting married.
14. It prevented several post-marital regrets.
15. Dual medical tests helped ensured someone got married to a medically fit partner.

16. The involvement of parents made it difficult for married couples to divorce each other for casual reasons.
17. The court filing made the relationship legally binding before the state.
18. It was difficult for any of the parties to be legally joined to another person while the other party was still alive.
19. It attracted both parental and church benedictions.
20. The post-marriage counseling was helpful when there were issues to be clarified or resolved immediately after the marriage.
21. Since many things were checked and clarified before the marriage, there was usually the absence of guilt.
22. It encouraged purity among youths in the church.
23. There was an opportunity to confirm spiritual compatibility and sameness of conviction, which made the marriage work out as desired. It is usually dangerous when both parties have a different spiritual belief on matters of eternal consequence. For example, intending couples should have the same conviction on divorce, child training, finances, etc.
24. Couples had ample opportunity to establish a foundation of good planning for their future.

DEMERITS OF CONSERVATIVE MODEL

1. Setting an age limit when people could commence their marriage journey was a good idea but has resulted in several complications. For example, a man wanted to propose to a lady but was told to wait until she attained a specified age. Unfortunately, the lady relocated to another city before the age set by the church. Another man in her new location proposed to her, and she agreed. The first man who wanted to marry her was offended. See details in the exceptional rule model.

2. Going through the pastor was a great idea. Nevertheless, several complications could erupt via this channel. I have seen a situation where the pastor had a vested interest in the lady that a man wanted to marry. Many factors could influence the pastor's decision. If the pastor does not want the man to marry the lady, he may also affect the process. I once had a conversation with someone who told me how he went to see his pastor about his leading. Incidentally, the lady in question was the pastor's daughter.

3. What happened at the pastor's level above may also occur at the MCU. There have been situations where the MCU acted in biased ways. Some have even been guilty of bending the rules for the church leaders' children.

4. Some MCU members have used their privileged decision-making capacity to avenge those who have offended them in the past.

5. When parents refused to approve of the marriage, intending couples could be denied the benefit of a church marriage.

6. Several ladies have been disappointed after marriage when they got to the man's house as the home's realities were way below their expectations. Some blamed their churches because they could not visit the man's house before they were married.

CHAPTER FIVE

Assumption Model

The only difference between this model and the conservative model was the omission of the medical test.

SCENARIO ONE

Richard and Rachael had been married for eight years. They have had four children with sickle cell anemia. Three died, and they are still battling with the last child. It has been a sorrowful marital voyage. Their church had also had a fair share of their pain.

SCENARIO TWO

Emmanuel and Ella got married. Their first child was diagnosed with HIV at birth. At this time, Emmanuel discovered he had contracted HIV from a previous relationship he was involved with. Ella also was confirmed positive. The end of the story was not pleasant.

ASSUMPTION MODEL

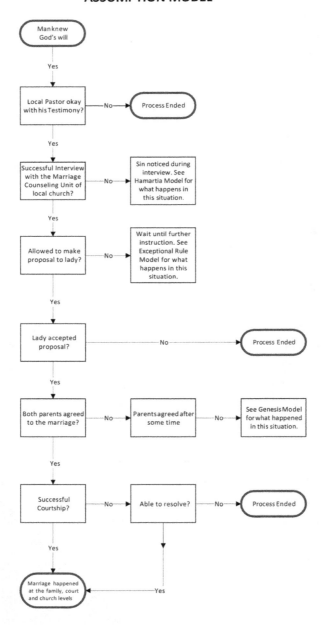

Fig. 8: Assumption Model Chart

MERITS OF ASSUMPTION MODEL

This model presents all the Conservative model's merits except those relating to the medical test information records.

DEMERITS OF ASSUMPTION MODEL

1. It did not promote total transparency.
2. It did not help intending partners to carry out an unbiased medical investigation.
3. In an instance, one of the parties did not provide a complete medical history. After the marriage, an underlying medical condition was revealed, which negatively affected the marriage.
4. Some couples had post-marital regrets traceable to insufficient knowledge of each other's medical history.

CHAPTER SIX

Independent Model

This model was adopted by some churches that had small congregants. The pastor coordinated all the affairs of the church, including marital issues. The only difference between this model and the conservative model was the omission of the MCU. However, the pastor tried to play all the roles of the MCU as well.

SCENARIO

Tom fell in love with Mary. Tom approached his pastor to share his marital intentions. His pastor told him to go and make his proposal to Mary. They agreed to marry each other. The pastor asked them to keep him in the loop as they plan towards their marriage.

INDEPENDENT MODEL

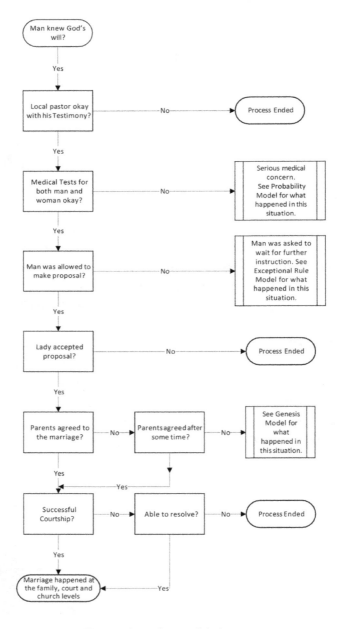

Fig. 9: Independent Model Chart

MERITS OF INDEPENDENT MODEL

1. Since small churches adopted it, the pastor was able to oversee relationship and marriage issues very well.
2. Some folks liked the idea that their church did not have any MCU, at they found it more comfortable to talk to their pastor alone.
3. Some said the proposal process was quicker and less regulated.
4. It attracted parental and church blessings.
5. A cordial relationship with their pastor made it easier to manage the courtship of intending couples.

DEMERITS OF INDEPENDENT MODEL

1. The pastor (sometimes in conjunction with his wife) may not be very knowledgeable medically, hence could not provide an all-round marriage advice to the intending couple.
2. Some instances of confusion, sensuality, and relationship break-ups occurred because marriage proposals from men to the ladies were less regulated.
3. Some instances of pastoral bias has also occurred.

CHAPTER SEVEN

Lacuna Model

Lacuna scenario happened between two people whose marriage started with a secret casual, unsupervised relationship but later came to the church to be joined together in marriage.

SCENARIO

Cuomo and Omar worked in the same organization. Often they go for coffee together. They soon became friends. Cuomo proposed to Omar after a few months. Omar was hesitant. They began dating for months but secretly. Nobody was aware of their affair. Soon, their relationship became intimate. After two abortions, Omar succumbed to marry him. Omar happened to be from a religious family, while his single mother raised Cuomo. According to Cuomo, his mum does not believe in religion. Omar's parents insisted that they had to be duly joined in the church. They were introduced to the church. Cuomo does not like attending church, but Omar made him go occasionally. After going through the catechism classes designed for intending couples, they got married in Omar's parent's church. After two years of their marital journey, Cuomo was caught cheating on Omar in a series of romantic affairs. Soon, they began having misunderstanding, which would last for days, sometimes weeks, and at other times months. After about three years of an enduring relationship, things fell apart between Cuomo and Omar as their relationship ended in divorce. Omar was left alone to cater for their two-year-old daughter. She was six months pregnant!

LACUNA MODEL

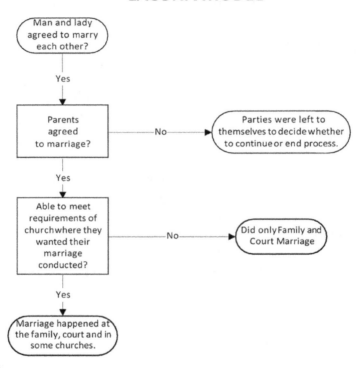

Fig. 10: Lacuna Model Chart

MERITS OF LACUNA MODEL

When parents agreed and the couples were able to meet church requirements, couples had family support, parental and church blessings.

DEMERITS OF LACUNA MODEL

Some of the couples who shared their experiences submitted that:

1. Church leadership was not involved in their relationship, marriage plans, and process. Therefore, they felt the absence of accountability to authority exposed them to several vulnerabilities and exploitation.
2. Some only realized how spiritually unprepared they were for the marriage after they got married.
3. Some people attributed the failure in their marriage to the absence of parental and spiritual mentorship and lack of someone they resort to for reconciliation before things went out of hand.
4. Some couples had untold post-marital regrets.
5. Pre-marital sex predisposed some couples to adultery. The lack of trust was common as couples' guilt of their pre-marital sexual sins continued to hunt them.
6. Marriage to an unbeliever became a dangerous adventure as the unbeliever was never predictable.

CHAPTER EIGHT

Elusive Model

This model was observed among churches where members married each other without leadership scrutiny. The notable issue here (in comparison with the conservative model) is that there was no official medical check, there was no MCU, and intending couples had the final say on the marriage plans. However, the pastor provided some guidance to the intending couples.

SCENARIO 1

Mary and Kerry filed for divorce after their third child's arrival while Cathy and Moses had been married for over 25 years and still enjoying their relationship. These two couples got married after the pattern of this model. They lived in the same country but had different experiences. In each situation above, both were Christians and got married because they fell in love with each other, after which they informed their pastors and parents of their marital intention. They both got married in the church.

MARRIAGE MODELS

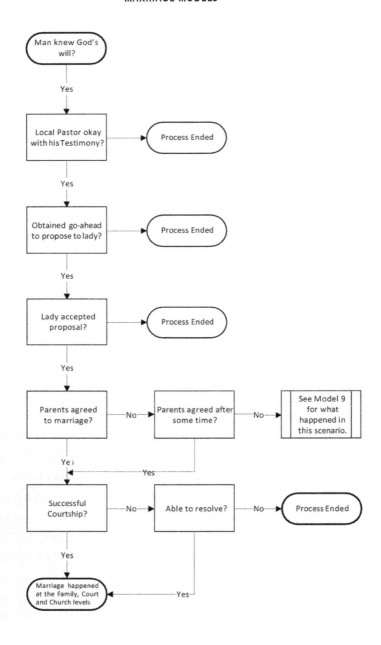

Fig. 11: Elusive Model Chart

MERITS OF ELUSIVE MODEL

1. One couple liked that there was no interference from too many people in their relationship.
2. Most of the couples under this scenario liked that their union had parental and church's blessings.

DEMERITS OF ELUSIVE MODEL

1. In one family, the medical incompatibility was only discovered after marriage.
2. The couples had the final say as pastoral guidance was not compulsory.
3. Several men made proposals to the ladies simultaneously, creating confusion for some ladies before marriage.
4. Carnality and relationship break-ups was commonplace experience in many relationships built on this model.

CHAPTER NINE

Traditional Model

C hristians whose parents had the final say regarding their marriage choices fall into this model. The families managed the general affairs that led to the marriage. The pastor/church was only informed when needed.

Everything under this model depended on what the families required. Medical tests were not mandatory, but the MCU provided counseling to intending couples towards their wedding.

In some cases, intending couples attended MCU in several churches due to one or more of the following reasons:

- The parents insisted that the wedding must happen in their church; hence they had to attend pre-marital classes there;
- The couple planned to join the church that conducted their wedding after their marriage, but they were asked to attend pre-marital classes as a condition;
- The couple were from separate denominations, and their respective churches required them to attend pre-marital classes.

SCENARIO 1

Steve prayed and felt led to Mary. Steve and Mary told their parents. Steve's parents told him to let them do their investigations about Mary's family before giving their consent. After the investigations, Steve's parents agreed to allow Steve to go ahead. Mary's parents informed her to consider Steve's proposal. Steve and Mary courted and got married 14 months afterward.

SCENARIO 2

Bobi's parents and Bekky's parents were family friends, and both families attended the same church. Both parents wanted their children to marry each other. Bobi's parents encouraged him to consider marrying Bekky. Bekky's parents tried to do the same. Both parents tried to arrange events that would bring Bobi and Bekky together to deepen their relationship. After some years, Bobi and Bekky got married.

SCENARIO 3

Charles was a wealthy guy but not saved. He approached Mr. and Mrs. John that he would like to marry their daughter – Ruth.

Ruth was a beautiful Christian lady. Several suitors were interested in Ruth, but her parents preferred Charles for obvious reasons – affluence and influence. Ruth's parents gave her to Charles for a substantial bridal price. Besides, he gave the parents a brand new car. Little did everyone know that Charles was into drugs and other unlawful businesses. Long story cut short, the Law enforcement agents were closing in on Charles, but he was at large. He was eventually arrested, and all his properties were confiscated. His bank accounts were frozen to offset his loots and embezzlements. After two years of marriage, Ruth was back to her parent's home with a baby and a pregnancy.

TRADITIONAL MODEL _ Scenario One

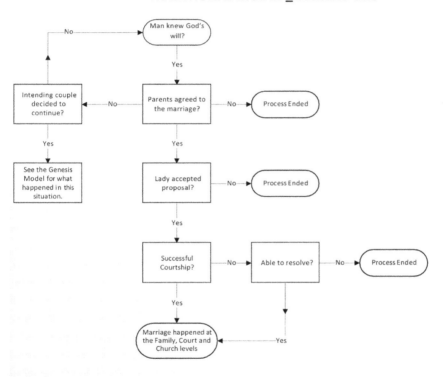

Fig. 12a: Traditional Model Chart

TRADITIONAL MODEL – Scenario Two

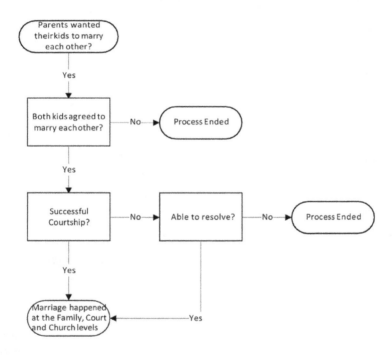

Fig. 12b: Traditional Model Chart

MERITS OF TRADITIONAL MODEL

1. Parental blessings.
2. There was no interference from too many people.
3. The proposal and feedback process was quick and easy.

DEMERITS OF TRADITIONAL MODEL

The following are a combination of submissions from couples based on their experiences:

1. Underlying risks followed some folks into their marriage unnoticed as families did not mandate medical tests.
2. Break up of the marriage were experienced in both relationships.
3. Lack of commitment to God's word and standard for the marriage covenant did not help the marriage relationships.
4. Unguided family influences resulted in several problems and spiritual derangements.
5. There was no guarantee that someone was not into several relationships without the parents' knowledge.

CHAPTER TEN

Free Range Model

The free-range model happened when intending couples dated and decided to marry each other without involving any parental or spiritual authority.

SCENARIO 1

Fred and Sarah started dating while in High School. They lived in different cities during the holidays but continued their relationship after college. They decided to tie the knot after dating each other for ten years.

SCENARIO 2

Blair and Selly met at work. They began their relationship casually but decided to get serious after a year of dating each other. They married two years later. However, they had premarital sexual interactions and even had to abort a couple of times. They bought a house together but later separated due to some conflicts.

FREE RANGE MODEL

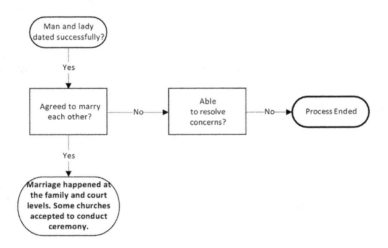

Fig. 13: Free-Range Model Chart

MERITS OF FREE-RANGE MODEL

1. Scenario 1 couple under this model seemed to be enjoying their marriage.

DEMERITS OF FREE-RANGE MODEL

Some other couples who shared their experiences submitted that:

1. The absence of spiritual authority, parental consent, and mentorship contributed to their marital problems.
2. The absence of accountability to authority exposed them to several vulnerabilities and exploitation.
3. Some marriages failed because they had nobody to whom they could resort to for reconciliation during misunderstandings.

CHAPTER ELEVEN

Probability Model

The probability scenario happened when intending couples had a notable medical problem or genotypic incompatibility, but they still wanted to marry each other.

SCENARIO ONE

Jude and Marge attended the same church right from their childhood days. Jude is now 27, and Marge had just celebrated her twenty-fifth birthday. They were both members of the church choir and have been friends for several years. They both fell in love with each other and believed that God made them for each other. Jude made the first move by informing their local pastor. They were asked to join the pre-marital counseling class. After six months, they began to get more serious about their wedding plans. At this point, they went for some medical tests and discovered both had AS Genotypes. It was a devastating development for the lovebirds. Nevertheless, the church advised them to end the relationship due to the associated risks, based on science. However, they decided to continue their relationship into marriage. All their four kids are sickle cell carriers (AS genotype). No SS!

SCENARIO TWO

Franklin and Judith were asked to provide the results of their medical tests before they could start their courtship. Every test requested by the church looks okay. However, Franklin had a surgery while young, which had damaged one of his testicles. They both agreed to marry and trust God for a miracle. After four years of waiting without a child, Judith began to have series of depression. She could not tell her family what the problem was. Their families thought Judith had problems with conception. She later said to Franklin that she regretted marrying him. She blamed herself, saying she did not pray enough to seek God for direction before saying 'yes' to him.

SCENARIO THREE

Mensah and Bibisca had a similar challenge as in scenario 1. They also decided to continue their relationship into marriage. However, They had four children, and four were SS. Three of the kids died in infancy. The last one died before reaching adulthood!

SCENARIO FOUR

Gift and Patience were already in love before Patience disclosed that she had lost her womb during an abortion she did several years earlier. They agreed to marry and adopt children. They are happily married.

PROBABILITY MODEL

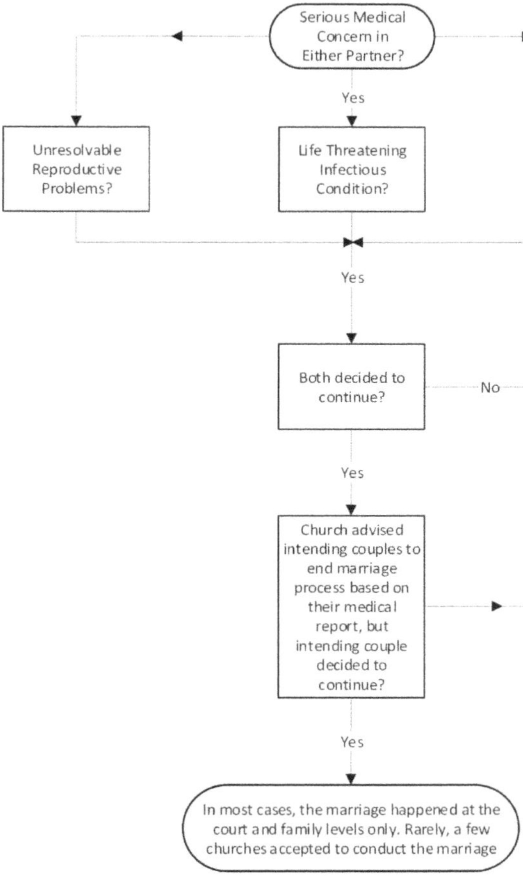

Fig. 14: Probability Model Chart

MERITS OF PROBABILITY MODEL

When those who prayed and felt led by God married and encountered no problems, it boosted the believers' faith.

DEMERITS OF PROBABILITY MODEL

Some folks experienced premature death of children, financial crisis due to medical expenses, and untimely death of either spouse when the underlying medical condition was infectious.

CHAPTER TWELVE
Genesis Model

G enesis scenario happened when the father of the lady or the man refused to agree to the marriage.

GENESIS MODEL SCENARIO

Joses felt led to Grace. They were already undergoing the conservative model in their church. However, Grace's father refused. The church did not grant them a go-ahead unless Grace's father agrees to the relationship.

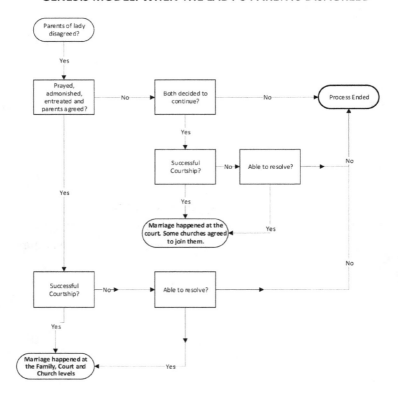

MARRIAGE MODELS

GENESIS MODEL: WHEN THE LADY'S PARENTS DISAGREED

Fig 15a: Genesis Model Chart

GENESIS MODEL: WHEN THE MAN'S PARENTS DISAGREED

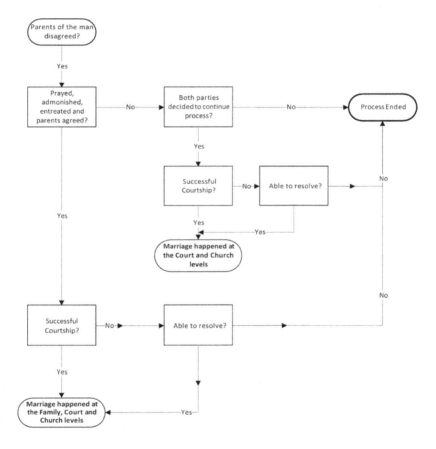

Fig 15b: Genesis Model Chart

MERITS OF GENESIS MODEL

1. Godly parental reasons saved intending couples from troubles and regrets.

DEMERITS OF GENESIS MODEL

1. Some marriages were delayed due to ungodly parental reservations and selfishness.
2. Distortion of God's perfect will for intending couples have been recorded when relationships were ended to please selfish parental demands.

CHAPTER THIRTEEN

Harmatia Model

These were situations when sexual sin was discovered between intending couples before the start of courtship or any time before the actual wedding ceremony.

SCENARIO ONE

Tom and Pat confessed during their pre-courtship interview to the MCU that they had been involved in sexual sin.

SCENARIO TWO

Evangel and Krista had courted under church authority for eight months. It was a few weeks to the wedding date. Post-courtship tests revealed that Krista had been seven weeks pregnant.

HAMARTIA MODEL

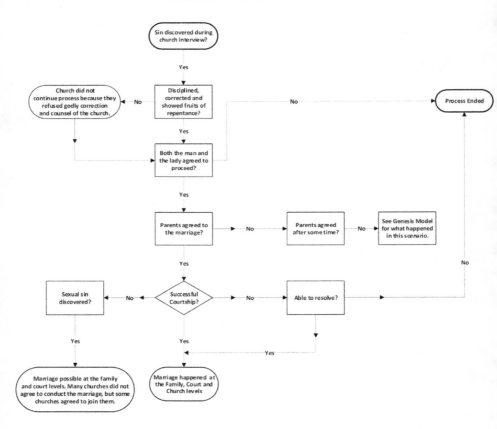

Fig. 16: Harmatia Model Chart

MERITS OF HARMATIA MODEL

1. The church's stand against sin helped others to run away from evil.
2. The church was able to help those who repented.
3. The church prioritized holiness above marriage.

DEMERITS OF HARMATIA MODEL

1. A nonchalance attitude towards correction was observed when the same standard was not being applied to everyone found guilty of the same sin.

CHAPTER FOURTEEN

Exceptional Rule Model

E xceptional rule happened when a man wanted to propose to a lady, but the church asked him to hold on because the lady was either not ready for marriage due to academic or any other reason.

The exceptional rule model was mostly encountered in churches that adopted the conservative model where specific age was set for people before getting married.

SCENARIO ONE

Anthony prayed and felt led to Maria. He went to the MCU for guidance but was told that he cannot propose to Maria because Maria is yet to complete her undergraduate classes.

Anthony was asked to wait until Maria finishes her studies so that Maria was not distracted from her studies. They later got married in the church.

SCENARIO TWO

Victor was 27 years old, and Vicky was 19. Victor is a serious Christian who had already completed his Masters and already working full time in an Engineering Firm. He was convinced Vicky was the "bone of his bone". He approached his church's MCU for guidance. However, the marriage process in his church aligns with the conservative model. In his church, females are not considered matured for marriage until they attain the age of 23 years. He was advised to let Vicky reach the age deemed appropriate by the church before talking to her.

Victor decided to wait. After two years, Vicky's family relocated to another city. Another man – George, in Vicky's new church, felt led to her and was allowed to propose to her. She had began a courtship with George before Victor revisited the church's MCU about his interest in Vicky. Victor's pastor contacted Vicky's new church, and they told him that she was already planning for her marriage. Victor was devastated, having waited for almost four years.

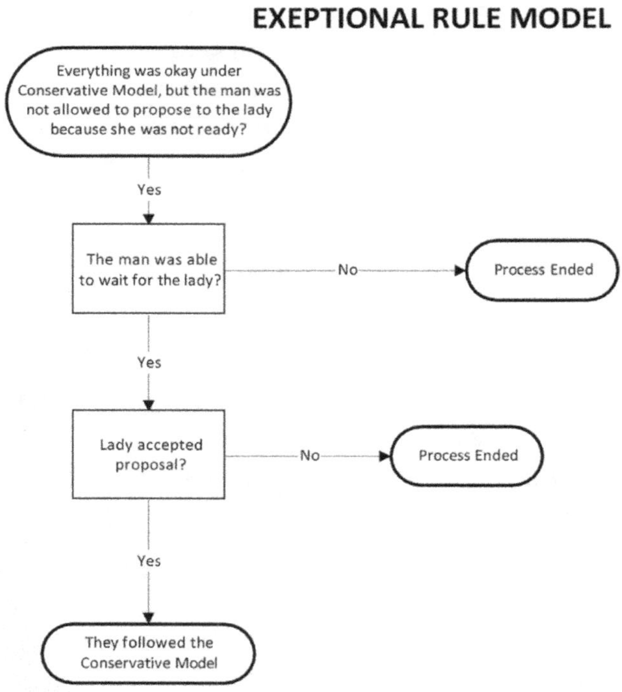

EXEPTIONAL RULE MODEL

Fig. 17: Exceptional Rule Model Chart

MERITS OF EXCEPTIONAL RULE MODEL

1. It precluded distraction from the lady's education.
2. It served as a test of conviction for some men.

DEMERITS OF EXCEPTIONAL RULE MODEL

1. Devastation of hearts, e.g., Victor's experience in scenario 2 of this model, resulted from poor church administration.

CHAPTER FIFTEEN

Compassionate Model

Compassionate scenario happened when a lady who was well-advanced in age felt that the man that God wanted her to marry was not coming forth.

Usually, the compassionate model was encountered in churches that adopted the conservative model where singles were not allowed to make marriage proposals, except they've gone through a formal church process.

SCENARIO

Beatrice was 37 years old. She was a committed member of the church. She had always dreamed of getting married to James. However, James was looking forward to getting married to Jennifer. Jennifer later got married to Kenny. James felt so disappointed and put any thought about marriage on hold. Beatrice was not sure if James would consider marrying her, but she felt in her heart that James was her perfect match in marriage. She approached the church's MCU for counseling. On compassionate ground, she was allowed to speak to James about her conviction and intentions.

COMPASSIONATE MODEL

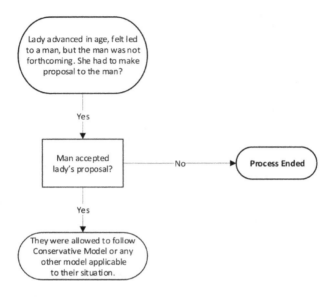

Fig. 18: Compassionate Model Chart

MERITS OF COMPASSIONATE MODEL

1. This model helped when the lady was sure, but the man was either confused, shy, or unsure.

DEMERITS OF COMPASSIONATE MODEL

1. It exposed the lady to carnality when the process was not well managed.
2. A man who married a lady out of sympathy and compassion later regretted his decision as his decision was only based on empathy and not on God's love or word.

CHAPTER SIXTEEN

Marital Spindles

For this cause shall a man leave his father and mother, and shall be joined unto his wife, and they two shall be one flesh (Eph. 5:31).

The subject of marriage is a significant topic of conversation within and outside the church. Many people have asked me several times—At what point does marriage take place? When is the right time to marry? What are the specific roles for couples in a marital relationship? These are all good questions, and there are no simple answers to any of them outside the Scriptures. Only the author of marriage could proffer the satisfactory remedies to problems that have remained unresolved in many homes and relationships.

Marriage is an intentional agreement to live together as husband and wife between one man and one woman (*not between a boy and a girl*).

What are the specific roles in marriage?

In every culture, marriage is a recognizable institution. God holds people accountable for what they do in marriage relationships. From creation, God created men to lead, hence the need for the woman's submissiveness. God also created the woman to be admired and loved. This is the secret of all happy marital relationships.

However, in addition to individual commitments to the specific roles stated in the Scriptures, both the husband and his wife must help each other achieve their God-given roles. Otherwise, marital bliss would be a mirage. The man must help his wife to be fulfilled in her God-given role of submissiveness. The wife also must help her husband to achieve his divine assignment to love. Whatever is lacking in one party must be supplied by the other. Love and submission are the two keys that open all other doors that lead to a successful marital adventure. It is childishness for the husband to say to the wife – Hey, only love is my duty. Once I love you, that is all. It will be immaturity for the wife to say Sir; submission is my duty; you are the one to love.

Unfortunately, this pointing of accusatory fingers to each other is commonplace even among church folks today. Since both husbands and wives are clear about their respective roles, they must join hands together to see that they are succeeding in these roles. That is the main point I am trying to emphasize here. No amount of prayers or counseling would suffice to restore peace and joy in any home where these two foundations are missing. Couples must work together as ONE to bring love and submission into their relationship and their home. Individual roles are recognized, but the weight and responsibilities that come with each role must not be left to each other to bear. Both parties must share the burdens. If you see any marriage successful, this is the secret.

This is how to fulfill the law of Christ in a marital relationship. The Scripture that says, *"...every man shall bear his own burden"* *also stipulates, "Bear ye one another's burdens, and so fulfil the law of* *Christ."* (Gal. 6:2,5).

What Is God's Purpose for Marriage?

To have a clear and moral understanding of marriage, the Holy Spirit illustrated marriage's concept using the relationship between Christ and the church. Let's look at what kind of relationship exists between Christ and the church.

1. Love relationship

One of God's foundational purposes of marriage is to provide a moral and legal platform for a man and a woman to express their love for each other. However, it is essential to note that there are four different types of love when talking about the love affair between a man and a woman: *eros*, *storge*, *phileo*, and *agape*. For God's purpose to be fulfilled in a marriage, all of these four kinds of love must be present. The absence of one or more of these loves is the root cause of many problems in marriages today. A marriage that is lacking in any one of *eros*, *phileo*, *storge*, or *agape* may only be endured and not enjoyed. A good and successful marriage must witness these four types of love. God has a purpose for each of these loves in marriage. Couples must demonstrate these four types of love to each other to fulfill God's purpose for their marriage. It is crucial to clarify that it is only in a legal marital union that all these four types of "loves" can be simultaneously enjoyed between a man and a woman without going into sin and displeasing the Lord.

Eros: Sex is sacred. Only within the purview of legal marital union can it be considered sinless. God created *eros* so that couples can enjoy the sexual aspect of their lives (1 Cor. 7:2). Any sex outside of wedlock is sinful and wicked. God hates sexual immorality. A believer must not be part of it in any way. It is evident in the Scriptures that all forms of sexual immoralities are sinful, including fornication (sex before marriage) and adultery (sex outside of marriage). As a believer, you must not allow it to happen in your room or house. Never should you excuse it in the life of another person so as not to become a partaker of other men's sins (Eph. 5:3–7).

Phileo: This is an affectionate and generous love that exists in friendship. Unfortunately, this is one of many reasons why Christian couples are not enjoying their marriage. They are not friends with each other. It is advisable not to marry out of sympathy or based on respect for a person's spirituality. While it is a notable fact that *phileo* may not be present at the start of a relationship, it must become real before you consummate the marriage. The period of courtship must accomplish this purpose in the lives of intending couples. If the courtship period fails to achieve it, there is no guarantee that marriage will do it. Those who marry out of sympathy live in apathy. Those who marry due to spirituality may realize too late that the person they married is human and not spirit. Intending couples must become genuine friends with each other to achieve God's purpose in their lives and marriage.

After marriage, any other friendship or tie stronger than the bond between a couple is an incorrect affair. They should discard such a relationship. It is wrong for the couple to be more bonded to either of their parents than to each other—God's perfect plan for couples is for them to become one flesh. No one should come in-between them.

Storge: This is an affectionate and unforced love witnessed between family members—between parents and children and between spouses. *Storge* binds the family together and helps families to realize and achieve God's perfect purpose. Parents must love their children and vice-versa. Children are God's heritage, and God wants them raised in love and without wrath. Children are placed under the parents for godly training and tutelage (Prov. 22:6). The successful upbringing of kids in the path of the Lord is God's reward (Psa. 127:3). The purposes of God would suffer when this is not happening in the family. Hence, there is a critical need to train children to follow the Lord.

Agape: This is the highest and most virtuous form of love. God expects spouses to surrender to each other to make their marriage work. *Agape* love is the currency that sustains conjugal bliss. Christ's death for the church was *agape*. He denied Himself of many things to come down to our level. He died to His right of being God to become a man and to die. It was afterward that He rose to gain everything He had lost. This analogy has the supreme wisdom for successful couples. God wants your marriage to succeed. To show your love for your partner, you must deny yourself of anything or anyone that would not make your marriage work, just as Christ did for the church.

2. Sacrificial relationship

God sacrificed His only begotten Son, Jesus. Christ gave His only life for the salvation of men. It is only man who seems to be finding some difficulty in loving God and Christ in return. Love is easier to sing in lyrics than demonstrated in sacrificial deeds. There would be no successful relationship without sacrifice. Once you are married, you will need to sacrifice something to please your spouse. In marriage, you must be willing to sacrifice your time, energy, resources, treasure, and everything you have with your partner. It is needful that you develop this virtue in your Christian life before marriage. Everybody needs someone's help. Through marriage, God enlarges our coast of helpers in life.

"For if they fall, the one will lift up his fellow: but woe to him that is alone when he falleth; for he hath not another to help him up. Again, if two lie together, then they have heat: but how can one be warm alone?" (Eccl. 4:10).

3. Collaborative relationship

God designed marriage for partnership. Spouses must join hands to fight their battles. Division begins when spouses have different views, and they decide to pursue separate visions to the detriment of their union. It is impressive to note in the Scriptures that one would only chase a thousand, but two would put ten thousand to flight! (Deut. 32:30). Also, *"Two are better than one; because they have a good reward for their labor"* (Eccl. 4:9). This truth has been tested and found to be real. Collaborating couples are successful couples.

Marriage should complement the weakness in a person's life by the strength of the partner. It is God's wisdom to hide in Eve that which is missing in Adam. God did that so Adam could find her as the help to meet the need in his life. The woman also will find in the man a fulfillment of her usefulness. If you are married, do not ever despise or abandon the help and satisfaction that God has designed for you in your spouse. If you are unmarried, you must seek the face of God to bring you into the realization of the bone of your bone and the flesh of your flesh. Marriage is a collaborative venture, so you must ensure you have prayed through the decision and that a collaborative partnership would be possible before you say yes to anyone in marriage. Some wives have built houses without the knowledge of their husbands. Yet, they live under the same roof, take pictures together, and attend the same church. I have seen this happen in several Christian families. It is always disheartening. In a particular situation, the wife would not contribute anything to support the nuclear family, but she built a mansion for her parents and siblings in another country. While this might sound ridiculous, it is the reality that exists in many homes.

There are many areas of collaboration. However, the financial partnership seems to be the most challenging aspect, where tension continues to wreck many families' foundations. God's purpose for couples entails economic collaboration. It is always more beneficial for couples to have a joint account or deal with each other in all honesty and truthfulness. Testimonies abound of how collaborative approaches in handling family matters have prospered many families.

4. Sincere relationship

The level of sincerity and openness practiced by couples goes a long way to determine how successful their relationship would be. Giving false impressions, claiming to have what you do not possess, and acquiring what your salary cannot afford are few of many reasons marriages fail. The level of insincerity among some couples is quite startling and unthinkable.

On one occasion, both the man and the woman already had children before they got married. They hid their past lives from each other throughout their courtship. Their parents were aware, but not their pastors. After they got married, the husband decided to open up to the wife. He told the wife he had a son living with his parents. The wife sighed in relief and told him her own story too. On hearing his wife's story, the man was mad. He asked the wife to leave his house. The husband's parents supported their son, insisting that the wife had to leave their son! Secrecy destroys relationships. There are many men and women whose spouses never knew how much they had in the bank.

God's purposes for many families are in jeopardy because of the absence of sincerity in the home. God wants couples to be sincere with each other, just as Christ was very transparent with the church. Every spouse should be able to say, like Christ, *"If it were not so, I would have told you."*

Productive relationship

One of the cardinal purposes of God for instituting marriage is fruitfulness. Barrenness is not in God's will for humanity. God's pronouncement upon marriage at his origin was productivity. "And God blessed them, saying, be fruitful, and multiply" (Gen. 1:22; 1:28).

This is God's original plan, and it is naturally possible only within the purview of a heterosexual relationship.

> And likewise also the men, leaving the natural use of the woman, burned in their lust one toward another; men with men working that which is unseemly, and receiving in themselves that recompence of their error which was meet. And even as they did not like to retain God in their knowledge, God gave them over to a reprobate mind, to do those things which are not convenient (Rom. 1:27–28).

A Christian should hold views that are not contrary to the word of God. If God is pro-life, all true Christians ought to be pro-life too.

Jesus said, "The thief cometh not, but for to steal, and to kill, and to destroy: I am come that they might have life, and that they might have it more abundantly" (John 10:10).

It is very scripturally concerning when anti-life and anti-productivity perspectives are being heralded and propagated by "Christians."

When does marriage take place?

Many youths have asked me this question. Is it at the family, court, or church level? Does the Bible provide clarifications for these questions?

I would like to first establish that marriage does not only happen between believers. An ideal marriage is a covenant between "a man and a woman." Also, there was no indication in the Scriptures that the man is to be "given" in marriage. It is usually the woman that is being "given" out during marriage. According to God's word, the man is to leave his father and mother, find a wife, and the woman is to be given to him by her parents, typically the father or his representative in the family.

"**For this cause** shall **a man leave his father and mother, and shall be joined unto his wife,** and they two shall be one flesh" (Gen. 2:24; Matt. 19:5; Mark 10:7; Eph. 5:31). "So then **he that giveth her in marriage** doeth well; but **he that giveth her not in marriage** doeth better" (1 Cor. 7:38).

Marriage could be said to have taken place at the point where all these requirements of scriptures are satisfied. To better appreciate the mind of God on marriage, we need to understand what happens at each of these stages.

At the family level, generally referred to as the traditional wedding (in some cultures) is where the families approve of the relationship and dowry (if applicable) is settled. At the court level, the union obtains a legal standing before the judicial system of the nation. Whereas at the church, there is an opportunity to bless the union by spiritual leaders. In many cultures, the church ceremony is not a mandatory step. Likewise, in the Bible, marriages only happened at the family level. There was no involvement of any cleric, clerk, or church.[4][5][6] The observance of church ceremonies started in 1563 and 1753 in the Catholic and Anglican churches, respectively. This further confirms that a marriage could still be acceptable to God without the church ceremony. I will liken the three stages—family, court, and church phases to moral, civil, and ceremonial approaches, respectively. Before God, a marriage relationship consummated at the family level could still be valid without the civil and ceremonial. I am not trying to undervalue the church ceremony. However, God recognizes the family phase as the most important. Among these three approaches to matrimony, the family stage is the most important to God, followed by the court phase. Specifically, for the marriage to be recognizable by the state, a person that has authorization to solemnize marriage, such as a court clerk or clerics of churches and religious denominations recognized under the Marriage laws of their state, must join couples together.

It is worthy of note that one of the most critical blessing upon the marriage is that of the parents. Even if the parents are not Christians, God approves of the blessings they place on their children. It is an essential condition to God that the woman's parent give their consent and hand over their daughter to the groom, and both the man and the woman must agree to become husband and wife.

And the servant brought forth jewels of silver, and jewels of gold, and raiment, and gave them to Rebekah: he gave also to her brother and to her mother precious things. And they did eat and drink, he and the men that were with him, and tarried all night; and they rose up in the morning, and he said, Send me away unto my master. And her brother and her mother said, Let the damsel abide with us a few days, at the least ten; after that she shall go. And he said unto them, Hinder me not, seeing the LORD hath prospered my way; send me away that I may go to my master. And they said, We will call the damsel, and enquire at her mouth. And they called Rebekah, and said unto her, Wilt thou go with this man? And she said, I will go. And they sent away Rebekah their sister, and her nurse, and Abraham's servant, and his men. And they blessed Rebekah, and said unto her, Thou art our sister, be thou the mother of thousands of millions, and let thy seed possess the gate of those which hate them. And the servant told Isaac all things that he had done. And Isaac brought her into his mother Sarah's tent, and took Rebekah, and she became his wife; and he loved her: and Isaac was comforted after his mother's death (Gen. 24:53-60, 66,67).

However, there are exceptional situations where intending couples may not want to involve their parents. In such circumstances, the court marriage alone would suffice.

I have seen several men who put away their wives after they became "born again." Their reasons were the same—they wanted a new marriage because they were married as unbelievers. Many have supported their claims with scriptures saying, "God winked at their times of ignorance." Such actions are wicked, and God is not the author of confusion, I must say.

Is marriage a covenant or an experiment?

An experiment is a trial or a test-run. It is like an investigation or an appraisal that is undertaken to make a finding. Hence, repeatability is a significant consideration in most experiments. To me, the marriage that God intended for man does not look like an experiment. According to the word of God, marriage is a covenant. God is the principal witness. It is a life-long commitment between a man and a woman *"because **the Lord hath been witness between thee and the wife of thy youth**, against whom thou hast dealt treacherously: yet is she thy companion, and* **the wife of thy covenant**" (Mal. 2:14).

Unfortunately, many couples today are experimenting and not covenanting. They marry, and after they have known each other, they end their experiment to begin another one. The Bible calls this practice sexual immorality, and God hates it. That is not God's purpose for the institution of marriage. First Corinthians 6:13 says, "Now the body is not for fornication, but for the Lord; and the Lord for the body."

CHAPTER SEVENTEEN

Important Clarifications For
The Married Seeking Divorce

B elow are several reasons why some Christians are considering divorce today. If you are looking for sound Bible-based clarifications and references, please read below.

Dowry accepted but returned to the couple/groom
(Common among Africans)

In some cultures, dowry is a typical traditional practice. Usually, the parents of the bride may return the bride price to the man. They might say they were not selling their daughter. It is a token of acceptance of the man and his gift. However, the father may decide to return the dowry to him as a token of love. It would be wrong to later say that the marriage is not valid because the dowry was returned to the bridegroom (in love). If the dowry were not accepted, the union would not have taken place in the first instance.

In some cultures, or jurisdictions where dowry is permitted by law, this is a traditional way of confirming that the bride's parents have agreed to give their daughter to the bridegroom. In many cases, the bride's parents may accept other gifts and return the money so as to remove the notion of "selling" their daughter. If the dowry price is returned to the groom, it is considered a kind gesture indicating acceptance of the groom as part of the family. It is not a rejection. Hence, this cannot be used as a basis for divorce in the future. I have intervened in some situations where the groom wanted to use this as an excuse to put his wife away. He claimed that since the dowry price was returned to him, it implies the marriage was invalid. If the return of the dowry indicated a rejection, why would such men continue to consummate the marriage? Such men are dubious and must not be allowed to have their way.

However, in some countries, dowry is illegal. It is important to check what is permitted in your country.

Those who want to divorce because they felt they did not do a church marriage

As explained above, marriage according to the Bible takes place when the following conditions are met:

- A father (or his representative) gives his daughter to a man as his wife.
- The lady agreed to be the man's wife.
- Both the bridegroom and the bride enters into a covenant to become husband and wife (either in the court, church or at the family level).
- It does not matter where the covenant takes place, provided the three conditions above have been met. Before God, the marriage has happened, and it remains valid until either the husband or wife is dead.

Those who want to divorce because they did only court marriage (no family involvement)

According to the Bible, if a couple is legally joined together in a court with an agreement to live together for the rest of their lives, God is witness. Even if they say they divorce afterward, God still sees them as one. They may be considered divorced before the state. However, in the sight of God, they remain husband and wife until death do them part (Rom. 7:1,2; 1 Cor. 7:39).

For Christians who wants to divorce on the basis of what Jesus said in Matthew 19:9

While the issue of marriage has been differently interpreted over the years by many churches and organizations, it is vital for the believer to understand what Jesus said. Today, many Christians are wrongly interpreting what Jesus said in this passage. The interpretation given to this passage by many Christians contradict Christ's stance and standard for marriage. These wrong or misleading teachings are due to a poor understanding of God's word. Hence, the need for you to consider what the Bible says with an open mind. Sometimes out of sympathy, safety reasons, or selfish concerns, married couples or individuals are given counsels which, in many ways, contradict the revealed word of God.

Please note that whenever the position of a denomination or the opinion of a priest, bishop, pastor, or a "reverend man of God" contradicts the words of Christ, the Bible encourages Christians to follow Jesus, who is the author and finisher of our proclaimed Faith (Heb. 12:2).

What should be the Christian standpoint on marriage? What did the Bible say regarding the subject of divorce and re-marriage? The Pharisees had asked Jesus a question whether a man could divorce his wife for every cause? The clarifications in Jesus' answer to this question, put forth by the Pharisees, would be the focus here.

Jesus, in response to their question, said,

"*And I say unto you, whosoever shall put away his wife, except it be for fornication, and shall marry another, committeth adultery: and whoso marrieth her which is put away doth commit adultery*" (Matt. 19:9).

Let me start by saying that this passage of scripture DOES NOT support divorce, and it cannot be a reason for divorce due to the following scriptural understandings:

(i.) The scripture never gave adultery as a condition for divorce; it instead says fornication.

Jesus said, "whosoever put away his wife **saving for the cause of fornication** causeth her to commit adultery." We must take note that the clause "except for fornication" only occurred in the book of Matthew. Let us consider the same discourse as recorded in other gospels.

> "And in the house his disciples asked him again of the same matter. And he saith unto them, Whosoever shall put away his wife, and marry another, committeth adultery against her. And if a woman shall put away her husband, and be married to another, she committeth adultery."
>
> **(Mark 10:10-12).**

"Whosoever putteth away his wife, and marrieth another, committeth adultery: and whosoever marrieth her that is put away from her husband committeth adultery" **(Luke 16:18).**

Why didn't Mark and Luke mention except for fornication?

It must be noted that the original audience in the book of Matthew were the Jews. In the Jewish culture, women must marry as virgins, with the evidence of a token of virginity. Whenever the husband could not find any evidence that the woman he married is

96

a virgin following his first sexual intercourse with her, the woman would be stoned to death as a penalty for her fornication (illicit sexual act before marriage).

"But if this thing be true, and the tokens of virginity be not found for the damsel: Then they shall bring out the damsel to the door of her father's house, and the men of her city shall stone her with stones that she die: because she hath wrought folly in Israel, to play the whore in her father's house: so shalt thou put evil away from among you" (Deut. 22:20,21).

Considering that the unfaithful woman had died as a consequent punishment for her fornication, the man could remarry because the marriage is only valid until either partner's death. I believe this is the correct clarification on this subject. Every other interpretation would lead to a contradiction of several other scriptures.

In both instances where Jesus' discourse on the issue of marriage and divorce was presented to the Jews in the Book of Matthew, the author was mindful to clarify the exception (Matt 5:32; 19:9) as it applied to his Jewish audience. You will never find that exception anywhere in the Bible.

Since this practice is only limited to the Jewish culture, the application cannot be generalized to the entire human race. Hence, the likely reason for the omission of the clause — "except for fornication"- in Mark and Luke's gospel accounts, whose original audience were not primarily Jewish.

(ii.) Even though adultery and fornication can have the same Greek root meaning — sexual immorality, they are not the same under specific contexts. For example, where both fornication and adultery appear in the same verse of scripture, they would not imply the same meaning as it is in Mathew 19:9 and Galatians 5:19. Hence, in Matthew 19:9, fornication and adultery have different specific connotations. It is intelligible and logical to understand that they would not have the same interpretation in such contexts. To give the same interpretation to both words in this context would render the verse meaningless. Fornication is an illicit sexual act that happens before marriage; therefore, it implies that a married person cannot commit fornication. He or she can only commit adultery. As explained, fornication is only possible before marriage. Whenever it occurs in the Jewish culture, and the husband discovers it on the first day of having sexual intercourse with his wife, the woman must die. Deuteronomy 22:13-21 clarifies this.

The guilty woman's death guaranteed the re-marriage of the innocent partner, NOT THE PUTTING AWAY. According to this verse – Matthew 19:9, divorce is NOT SCRIPTURALLY POSSIBLE (since, in this context, fornication is not possible among married couples).

Hence, Jesus did not give any permission for divorce; instead, He referred the Pharisees back to God's original plan and emphasized the validity of the marriage relationship until death do them part. "Wherefore they are no more twain, but one flesh. What therefore God hath joined together, **let not man put asunder**" (Matt. 19:6). Jesus made it clear that anyone whose spouse is still alive and marries another person is committing adultery.

"But I say unto you, that whosoever shall put away his wife, **saving for the cause of fornication**, causeth her to commit adultery: and **whosoever shall marry her that is divorced committeth adultery**" (Matt. 5:32).

"And I say unto you, whosoever shall put away his wife, except it be for fornication, and shall marry another, committeth adultery: and whoso marrieth her which is put away doth commit adultery" **(Matt. 19:9)**.

Once a leaving and cleaving has occurred in accordance with God's pattern for man, God has witnessed the marital union, and it remains valid before God until death ends the relationship. According to Scripture, death is the only factor that puts an end to a marriage before God, **not man**. Couples are not allowed to divorce each other. Apostle Paul also said the same thing (Rom. 7:2,3; 1 Cor. 7:39). Any varied opinions from Christ's will not be safe to consider. This is Jesus' final verdict on this issue. It does not matter who is involved. God does not authorize confusion.

(iii.) Jesus told us that He and His Father are one (John 10:30). God, the Father, also testified again and again that He is well pleased with the Son (Matt. 3:17; 17:5). Hence, I believe that God and Jesus cannot contradict each other. If God says He hates putting away (divorce) according to Malachi 2:15-16, Jesus Christ cannot permit it in Mathew 19:9.

Perhaps you might say Jesus contradicted some Old Testament laws. Would that not mean a contradiction between God's law and Christ? Of course not! A careful study of the scriptures consistently showed that God only removed an Old Testament condition if there is a replacive provision for it in His offer of Salvation to humanity through Jesus Christ in the New Testament. For example, in the Old Testament, God said, "eye for an eye" and "tooth for tooth" (Exod. 21:24), but Christ came and said it should no more be so. Is this a contradiction? No. There is no contradiction between God and Jesus. Jesus said, "it will no more be so" now because His life has become a ransom for the "eye," "tooth," and "foot" (Matthew 5:38). However, in the case of marriage, divorce, and re-marriage, Jesus categorically referred all men back to God's original, perfect, and only will, which is, "as it was in the beginning"! (Matt. 19:8). Jesus understood what He was saying when He referred the Pharisees back to what God said in the beginning because He was there with God in the beginning. You must always note that Jesus was there in the beginning with the Godhead when marriage was instituted. Hence, we must listen to Him.

"In the beginning was the Word, and the Word was with God, and the Word was God. The same was in the beginning with God. All things were made by him; and without him was not any thing made that was made" (John 1:1-3). The Godhead comprises of God, Jesus, and the Holy Spirit, and they are ONE in everything.

"For there are three that bear record in heaven, the Father, the Word, and the Holy Ghost: and these three are one" (1 John 5:7).

(iv.) Often, people quote Paul's writing as a support for divorce! I will like all Christians to get it clear that Apostle Paul never supported divorce. Paul said in 1 Corinthians 7:10, "And unto the married **I command, yet not I, but the Lord**, let not the wife depart from her husband: but and if she depart, let her remain unmarried, or be reconciled to her husband: and let not the husband put away his wife." It is very clear from this passage that both Jesus and Paul DID NOT SUPPORT divorce.

(v.) 1 Corinthians 7:11 came up with a marital scenario where one of the couple is not a believer. The scripture says, "But and if she departs," **not if she divorces.** This scripture addresses an abnormal situation, where the unsaved wife does not want to stay with the saved husband anymore. No doubt, this is a deviation from God's desire for couples. However, God's word to the one who chooses to depart from her spouse is clear in this scripture – "**Let her remain unmarried or be reconciled to her husband: and let not the husband put away his wife.**"

In the root meaning, the word "to put away" means to divorce. This means that even if she departs or moves out of the husband's house, God still sees them as husband and wife. As noted in 1 Cor. 7:11, the husband is not allowed in the Scriptures to divorce his wife. Hence divorce is not the option here too. According to Paul's writings, the second marriage is not a Christian option at all, if the other partner is still alive.

"For the woman which hath an husband is bound by the law to her husband so long as he liveth; but if the husband be dead, she is loosed from the law of her husband. So then if, while her husband liveth, she be married to another man, she shall be called an adulteress: but if her husband be dead, she is free from that law; so that she is no adulteress, though she be married to another man" (Rom. 7:2,3).

"The wife is bound by the law as long as her husband liveth; but if her husband be dead, she is at liberty to be married to whom she will; only in the Lord" (1Cor. 7:39).

(vi.) You might be wondering, what did Apostle Paul mean when he said, "but to the rest speak I, not the Lord…" (1 Cor. 7:12-16)? Does it mean that this portion of the scripture is of Paul's private interpretation or opinion? To assume that Paul was only suggesting his idea, in this case, will render this segment of scriptures uninspired. If that notion is true, then it would be a contradiction to the inspirational basis for ALL scriptures, bringing the entire Bible into crumbles.

"Knowing this first, that **no prophecy of the scripture is of any private interpretation**" (2 Peter 1:20).

"**All scripture is given by inspiration of God**, and is profitable for doctrine, for reproof, for correction, for instruction in righteousness" (2 Tim. 3:16).

Recall that the question presented to Jesus by the Pharisees was solely on divorce. However, there were several marital anomalies that came up among the Gentiles during Paul's days that were never raised or addressed in the gospels. These marital complications common among the Gentiles were not the problems of the Jews when Jesus was addressing the issue of marriage and divorce with the Jews. Hence the need for Apostle Paul by the Holy Spirit's inspiration to throw more light on these new developments. Apostle Paul was only buttressing what Jesus had earlier taught on marriage. How can we affirm that Apostle Paul wrote this out of the inspiration of the Holy Spirit?

Apostle Paul began to address this particular case in 1 Corinthians 7:12-14, and he used the phrase — **Let him not divorce her (verse 12); let her not divorce him (verse 13).** Paul's statement was in perfect harmony with the words of Jesus Christ about marriage and divorce. Paul had no contradictory opinion on Christ's verdict. Paul also confirmed that the inspiration he received on this subject to be from the Holy Spirit (1 Cor. 7:40). Thus, we can say that Christ's word is fulfilled as it is written, *"Howbeit when he, the Spirit of truth, is come, he will guide you into all truth: for **he shall not speak of himself;** but whatsoever he shall hear, that shall he speak: and he will shew you things to come. **He shall glorify me: for he shall receive of mine, and shall shew it unto you.** All things that the Father hath are mine: therefore said I, that he shall take of mine, and shall shew it unto you"* (John 16:13-15).

Hence, the Holy Spirit can be said to have taken from that which is of Christ and showed it unto Paul. Moreover, the Holy Spirit cannot be said to be glorifying Jesus if He tells Paul something that contradicts what Jesus said. Anyone who claims to have a revelation from a spirit, which contradicts the revealed words of Jesus must be referring to another spirit (Gal.1:8).

Please note the following points regarding 1 Corinthians 7:13 and 15:

(i.) **A brother or a sister is not under bondage in such cases: but God hath called us to peace.** Building on the preceding verses, "a brother or a sister is not under bondage in such cases": does not and CANNOT mean not under bondage from re-marrying as that would be contradictory to God's word that says that they are one as long as they are both alive. The scripture did not say if the unbelieving divorces. Instead, the scripture says, "if the unbelieving depart, let him depart," and not if the unbelieving divorce." It only implies that he or she is not under bondage to stay with the unbelieving partner. The departure referred to in this verse does not mean divorce, which is why Paul's final advice remains: **Let her remain unmarried or be reconciled**

to her husband, which shows that divorce did not take place, despite the separation or departure. Again, **divorce is not the option here too**.

It is sad to see and hear many teachers, preachers, and authors wrongly interpret this passage over the years.

(ii.) As evident in the Scriptures, the liberty to let him/her depart does not give the freedom to divorce or get married to another man or woman.

(iii.) It is noteworthy that this passage is addressing a marriage between a believer and an unbeliever. Believers are admonished not to be unequally yoked together with an unbeliever who may decide to depart at will.

I have heard several couples who feel there is nothing wrong with marital breakdowns. To them, it was not an unexpected circumstance.

An unbeliever may decide to leave the marriage relationship at any time because he or she is not under the guidance of the Holy Spirit and the control of God's word. Many Christians face this unpleasant repercussion today because they went outside of God's will and got unequally yoked together with an unbeliever in marriage.

Be ye not unequally yoked together with unbelievers: for what fellowship hath righteousness with unrighteousness? and what communion hath light with darkness? And what concord hath Christ with Belial? or what part hath he that believeth with an infidel? And what agreement hath the temple of God with idols? for ye are the temple of the living God; as God hath said, I will dwell in them, and walk in them; and I will be their God, and they shall be my people. Wherefore come out from among them, and be ye separate, saith the Lord, and touch not the unclean thing; and I will receive you. And will be a Father unto you, and ye shall be my sons and daughters, saith the Lord Almighty (2 Cor. 6:14-18).

(iv.) When the marriage between a believer and an unbeliever is valid, a subsequent conversion to Christianity or otherwise of either of the couple will not nullify their marital vows and conjugal duties towards each other. According to God's word, the saved partner should live in such a way that the unbelieving partner may come to the knowledge of Christ. A saved spouse should be committed to the salvation of his or her partner. It is more disturbing to see some pastors divorce their wives and "marry" another woman. In my considered opinion, if people believe the Bible as God's word, they should practice what it says (Luke 6:46). If a pastor would not give up on the souls of men and women outside his household, why should he give up on the wife of his youth? Why should he give up on the one who he once claimed to be the love of his life?

"For the unbelieving husband is sanctified by the wife, and the unbelieving wife is sanctified by the husband" (1 Cor. 7:14a).

Moreover, it would also be incorrect to conclude that an unbelieving spouse cannot be born-again or restored to his or her partner.

(vi.) Jesus said in response to this question—"In the beginning it was not so"! Who then were there in the beginning? John 1:1,14 says, "In the beginning was the Word, and the Word was with God, and the Word was God...and the Word was made flesh, and dwelt among us, (and we beheld his glory, the glory as of the only begotten of the Father,) full of grace and truth."

Due to the people's hardened hearts, Moses gave them a divorce certificate (Matt. 19:8). However, the fact that Moses gave the instruction did not make it the word of God! Christ's referral back to God's original intention invalidates Moses' certificate of divorcement. Hence, Christ's statement makes it very clear that divorce is not God's will. By implication, Jesus clarified that the idea of issuing a certificate of divorce was Moses' and not of God.

You might want to ask, were Moses' words not inspired? One thing is clear in Deuteronomy 24:1 where the bill of divorcement was first mentioned — Moses did not say he received the instruction about the certificate of divorcement from God. According to Scriptures, it was something that Moses did out of pressure from the people. Even though Moses told the people to issue the bill of divorcement, Jesus corrected this error (Matt. 19:8). There are other mistakes of several servants of God that were highlighted in the Scriptures for our admonition (1 Cor. 10:11). They are not instructions to obey or lifestyles to emulate. Such accounts are historical narratives and facts that should make believers tread cautiously rather than use such stories as a license to repeat such sins.

The Holy Spirit cannot contradict Jesus. Whenever the words, opinion, or decision of any man, prophet, or any other authority contradicts the words of Jesus, a Christian must follow Christ (Heb. 13:2). DEATH is the only thing that ends a correct marriage relationship. No man is ordained to dissolve that which God has joined.

"What therefore God hath joined together, let not man put asunder" (Mark 10:9).

(vii.) From the words of Jesus on marriage in Matthew 19:7-9, the writing and issuing a divorce certificate to a woman is not God's choice. Any man who gives his wife a divorce certificate exposes her to adultery. That is the same as giving her a license to go and commit adultery with other men. That certificate in her hand is evidence to show other men that her husband allows them to sleep with her. All scriptures condemn this as an abominable act before God. Jesus' final verdict was clear—"But I say unto you, That whosoever shall put away his wife, saving for the cause of fornication, causeth her to commit adultery: and whosoever shall marry her that is divorced committeth adultery" (Matt. 5:32). In this context, the use of fornication refers to illicit sexual act before marriage. I have explained why a married person cannot commit this sin of fornication that Jesus referred to in the Book of Matthew.

Mark's record also confirms that both the Pharisees and Jesus' Disciples were clear about the position of Jesus. The Pharisees only wanted an excuse to grant them the liberty to divorce their wives. **Jesus answered them in the context of their question and how it related to their culture.**

And the Pharisees came to him, and asked him, Is it lawful for a man to put away his wife? tempting him. And he answered and said unto them, What did Moses command you? And they said, Moses suffered to write a bill of divorcement, and to put her away. And Jesus answered and said unto them, For the hardness of your heart he wrote you this precept. But from the beginning of the creation God made them male and female. For this cause shall a man leave his father and mother, and cleave to his wife; and they twain shall be one flesh: so then they are no more twain, but one flesh. What therefore God hath joined together, let not man put asunder (Mark 10:2-9).

However, the disciples needed more clarification on this subject, and they asked Jesus for a more detailed explanation when they got home.

As shown in the above Scripture, the question brought to Jesus by the Pharisees was one-sided, relating only to when a man could put his wife away. They did not ask for when a woman could put away her husband. This time, in the house with His disciples, Jesus went beyond the situation of a man putting away his wife. He added the context of the woman to the answer. He told them neither the man nor the woman was permitted to terminate the marriage covenant and marry another person.

And in the house his disciples asked him again of the same matter. And he saith unto them, whosoever shall put away his wife, and marry another, committeth adultery against her. And if a woman shall put away her husband, and be married to another, she committeth adultery (Mark 10:10-12).

Whosoever putteth away his wife, and marrieth another, committeth adultery: and whosoever marrieth her that is put away from her husband committeth adultery (Luke 16:18).

From the entire gospels, both divorcing or getting married to a divorced person are not approved.

In the Scriptures, the position of Jesus on divorce was clear to both the Pharisees and His disciples. The narrative in Luke's book was also in agreement with what was recorded by Matthew and Mark.

John did not record the questions of the Pharisees. Nevertheless, he recorded the position of Jesus on adultery. The judgment of Jesus in John 4 is quite instructive when He met a woman who has had five husbands. If adultery ends a marriage, it would have nullified the Samaritan woman's first marriage. It is eye-opening that Jesus invalidated the legality of her multiple mariages. Note that Jesus did not recognize her current relationship as a correct marriage. It is either this woman had never had a correct marriage, or she left her first husband and began to sleep around with different men. The fact remains that if you leave your spouse, any subsequent marriage to another person while your partner lives will be equivalent to adultery.

For thou hast had five husbands; and he whom thou now hast is not thy husband: in that saidst thou truly (John 4:18).

For those who want to divorce their spouse because of adultery

It is essential to recognize in Matthew 19:9 that Jesus did not refer to adultery. He differentiated between the two. In that passage, He only referred to fornication, as I have explained above.

Under the Mosaic law, death was the penalty for adultery and rape, as shown in the table below.

SITUATION	CONSEQUENCE/PENALTY	BIBLE REFERENCE
Adultery with another man's wife	**Death** of both the man and the woman	Lev. 20:10
Adultery between a man and a married woman	**Death** of both the man and the woman	Deut. 22:22
Fornication by a lady before marriage, discovered by the man on the first night of their marriage	The man is to report the case to the city elders. The woman will be stoned to **death.**	Deut. 22: 13-21
Adultery/fornication between a man and a woman that is not married but is already engaged to another man	**Death** of both the man and the woman (because she did not cry out)	Deut. 22:23,24
Rape of a virgin that is already engaged to another man	**Death** of the man only (because the woman cried out)	Deut. 22:25-27
Fornication between an unmarried man and a virgin that is not engaged to any man	The man shall be asked to marry her if the lady's father agrees (accepts the dowry of a virgin from him).	Deut. 22:28,29
Unverifiable allegation or suspicion of adultery from the husband against his wife	Head-shaving and drinking of the "bitter water."	Num. 5:18-30
Loss of affection by the man for the woman he had married.	Bill of divorcement. Jesus said this bill was Moses' idea, not God's. It was one-sided to satisfy the hardness of the heart of the man only. There was no consideration for when the woman finds uncleanness in the man. In the Old Testament, it was noted that the bill of divorcement could cause the land to sin. Jesus said anyone who does this in the New Testament would be committing adultery.	Deut. 24:1-4 Matt. 19:8,9

Table 2: Scriptural Overview of Adultery and Fornication

However, in the New Testament, all Scriptures confirm that God's law concerning adultery is still in force. Adultery remains a very serious sin before God, either it is done by a man or a woman (Matt. 5:27,28,32; 19:9, 18; Mark 10:11,12,19; Luke 16:18,20; John 8:1-11; Rom. 2:22; 13:9; Gal. 5:19-21; Heb. 13:4; James 2:11; 2 Peter 2:14; Rev. 2:22). However, in contrast to the Old Testament, death is no longer the penalty for adultery. It is important to remember at this point that Jesus said he did not come to nullify the law but to fulfill it (Matt. 5:17-19). However, the grace that anyone who believes in Jesus obtains sets him or her free from the law (Rom.

6:14; 7:4-5; Gal. 2:21). Is there a contradiction in the Scriptures? No. Which law did grace render null and void?

There are three laws in the Old Testament – ceremonial, civic, and moral. Jesus came to fulfill the ceremonial laws, representing all the sacrifices and physical cleansings that men do to approach God. Yet, Jesus did not nullify both the civil and moral laws. The fact that you become a Christian does not exonerate you from the judicial laws of your state. Adultery is a crime in most civilized societies. Hence, the civil law of the land where someone commits adultery may still be applied as stipulated by their constitutions and criminal laws. God also being a moral God promised that He will still judge the adulterer and adulteress (Heb. 13:4). The prerogative of that judgment is in God's hands. Nevertheless, the Scriptures gave room for forgiveness and reconciliation for those who repent (Luke 18:10-14; John 4:16; 8:1-11; 1 Cor. 7:11). Only the unrepentant adulterers and adulteresses are promised eternal doom in hell (Gal. 5:19-21; Rev. 1 Cor. 6:9; Rev. 2:22).

Therefore, the New Testament believers must understand that no Scripture supports any of the following as a reason for divorce:

- Adultery
- Fornication (with child) – a situation where your spouse had a child with another person before your marriage
- Fornication (without child) – a situation where your spouse had sex with another person before your marriage, but no child was involved.
- Risk of life – situations that may include diabolism, abuse, violence, fighting, etc.
- Parental dissatisfaction with your spouse
- Loss of affection/lack of respect, love, or submission by either of the spouses for/to the other

- Loss of affection/ lack of respect, love, or submission by both spouses for/to each other

Separation, Not Divorce

According to the Scriptures, in certain situations (e.g., where there is risk of life), a separation may be okay, **without remarriage to another person.** However, instead of remaining separated, the Bible admonishes "separated couples" to reconcile with each other (1 Cor. 7:11).

If a partner goes into adultery in the New Testament, God said He would judge (Heb 13:4). He did not tell the faithful husband or wife should decide what is good for him or her. Judgment and vengeance belong to God. God has promised—"I will repay." However, the prerogative of how he would repay lies with Him. To take judgment or vengeance into our hands would be a sin.

Dearly beloved, avenge not yourselves, but rather give place unto wrath: for it is written, Vengeance is mine; I will repay, saith the Lord (Romans 12:19).

The options given to the faithful partner in 1 Cor. 7 is clear – separate and remain single or be reconciled.

But and if he/she departs, let him/her remain unmarried or be reconciled to his wife/her husband: and let not the husband put away his wife (1 Cor. 7:11).

God commands us to honor our marriages. If anyone put his spouse away, he/she is not only dishonoring that marriage, but also God who gave the command (Heb 13:4). Jesus made it clear that anyone who divorces his/her spouse is giving occasion for adultery (Matt. 5:32; 19:6; Mark 10:11,12; Luke 16:18).

The only institution that God used in the Scriptures to illustrate the relationship between Christ and the Church is the Marriage Institution (Rev. 21:2,9). Hence, our marriage should point us to God and not otherwise. We all know that Christ is married to the church. Christ's union to His body (the Church) is permanent. Note that a single Christian is not the CHURCH. Hence, a Christian may fall away if he/she reverts into sin, but the entire church of Christ cannot be lost. Jesus Christ wants us to understand that the marriage covenant is valid till death. **In the Old Testament**, God said He hates divorce (Mal. 2:16). **In the New Testament**, Jesus did not approve divorce (Matt. 19:9). **Today**, the Holy Spirit cannot speak to the contrary.

Annulment, Not Divorce

According to Jesus, eunuchs are not supposed to marry. If anyone is DECEIVED into marrying a eunuch, the person who feels deceived may contact the authority that joined them based on what Jesus said in Matthew 19:11,12.

> *But he said unto them, All men cannot receive this saying, save they to whom it is given. For there are some eunuchs, **which were so born from their mother's womb**: and there are some eunuchs, **which were made eunuchs of men**: and there be eunuchs, **which have made themselves eunuchs for the kingdom of heaven's sake**. He that is able to receive it, let him receive it.*

SCENARIO 1

A lady who did not have a reproductive organ got married to a man in a church. After the wedding, the man discovered and cried out to the church. The church leadership annulled the marriage. They believed a eunuch who wants to marry must let the intending partner know of his/her medical condition before the marriage.

SCENARIO 2

A man who was a eunuch went to join a particular church and got married to a lady. After the marriage, the lady was worried as the man could not perform sexually. She later discovered the man's condition and was heartbroken. It took several months before the man opened up. Their church was later informed, but the lady decided to stay in the marriage due to the stigma.

Template Of Courtship Conversations
For Intending Couples

COURTSHIP CONVERSATIONS

Date:　　　　　　　**Time**:　　　　　　　**Location**:

Agenda – Family background

1. Discuss your family background
2. Tell each other about your paternal sides (as much as you know).
3. Tell each other about your maternal sides (as much as you know).
4. List members of your nuclear family. You may want to let each other know a bit of the peculiarities of each member of your family.
5. Discuss important things about your personal lives.
    a. Honestly share your past lives before meeting Christ
    b. Share the testimonies of your salvation experiences (place, any relevant person to note at this point in your lives, remarkable restitutions done, etc.)
    c. Share remarkable landmarks in your Christian so far.
6. Growing up (e.g., upbringing, vocation, etc.)
7. Any other information

Submissions from Intending Groom

Submissions from Intending Bride

Agreements from current conversation (if any)

Concerns from current conversation (if any)

Prayer Points from the current conversation

Suggested Scriptures Based on Focus of Conversation:

Isaiah 28:16; 1 Cor. 3:10-15

Keys to productive Bible Discussions: As much as possible, Bible discussion should flow with the stage you are in the relationship. It may be helpful to focus on any of the following areas:

- Making Christ the foundation of everything you do
- Building trust and confidence in God

Next Meeting

Date | Time, Location

COURTSHIP CONVERSATIONS

Date: Time: Location:

Agenda – Educational and career issues

1. Education Attainment
    a. List schools attended so far.
    b. Itemize Degrees acquired till date.
    c. Discuss Degrees in-view or those you desire to have.
2. Career Path
    a. Discuss work experience
    b. If any of you is not working, discuss possible career opportunities
    c. Discuss everything likely to affect marriage plans from a career perspective
3. Professional Aspirations
    a. Discuss any study intentions that you intend to pursue after marriage
    b. Any plan to change career?
    c. Business intentions?
    d. Etc.
4. Notable Success and Failures Stories
    a. School
    b. Ministry
    c. Sports
    d. Church
    e. Professional
    f. Family
    g. Etc.

Submissions from Intending Groom

Submissions from Intending Bride

Agreements from current conversation (if any)

Concerns from current conversation (if any)

Prayer Points from the current conversation

Suggested Scriptures Based on Focus of Conversation:

Rom. 12:11; 1 Cor. 9:24-27; Prov. 22:29

Keys to productive Bible Discussions: As much as possible, Bible discussion should flow with the stage you are in the relationship. It may be helpful to focus on any of the following areas:

- What you can do to have a beautiful, bright, and befitting future
- Opportunities to explore
- Etc.

Next Meeting

Date | Time, Location

COURTSHIP CONVERSATIONS

Date: Time: Location:

Agenda – Financial issues

1. Finances
   a. Sincerely discuss your current income opportunities and budgets
   b. Discuss what your budget might look like after marriage (things may change, but it is good to have a discussion around personal and other financial commitments that may after family budget after marriage, as much as you can foresee)
   c. Discuss how you would like to make a budget for the family (e.g., at the beginning of every month, every week, etc.)
   d. Discuss potential sources of income for your budgeting plans after marriage and be sure your intentions are feasible.
   e. Discuss savings plan (e.g. what percentage of your current income goes into savings. Etc.).
2. Bank Accounting
   a. What are your views about having a common bank account after marriage?
      i.   Itemize the merits
      ii. Discuss the demerits
   b. Will you like to continue to use our individual accounts after marriage?
3. Other areas of finance to discuss
   a. Views on tithing and offering – takes priority over other expenses
   b. Perspectives on how to manage family upkeep
      a. Food
      b. Where to stay (Rent, etc.)
      c. Car maintenance/transport
   c. How often do you want to be buying clothing?
   d. How do you want to manage house maintenance – e.g., furniture, building project.

e. Investment for future e. g., what are the investments you are interested in? You may book appointments with your bankers to decide the best financial advice that suits you. Family investments must be made **with much carefulness.**
f. Financially supporting churches, outreaches, ministries, missionaries, etc.
    a. Perspectives on making pledges (individually or seek each other's consent?)
    b. Discuss how you may want to manage if certain requests/issues come up after you have made the family budget for the month?

4. Discuss some tips for handling money in the home
For example:
    a. Will family togetherness and oneness more important to you over financial issues?
    b. Do either of you have concerns about working hard (and smartly), but living simply?
    c. How serious do you take honesty, fairness, and generosity? You may draw out a rating criterion over 10.
    d. What are you currently doing now that might enhance the early payment of bills to avoid being charged for late fees?
    e. How would you prioritize one another's needs when making budgetary plans?
    f. Prayer for divine provisions and Holy Ghost directions in money spending

5. Discuss the pitfalls to avoid. You may want to discuss how you will avoid:
    a. Careless spending
    b. Buying things that are too expensive
    c. Loans/borrowing/spending from credit cards
    d. Live within your income
    e. Impulsive buying
    f. Making vows or doing charitable deeds to people without the knowledge of each other
    g. Independent financial projects

Submissions from Intending Groom

Submissions from Intending Bride

Agreements from current conversation (if any)

Concerns from current conversation (if any)

Prayer Points from the current conversation

Suggested Scriptures Based on Focus of Conversation:

Rom. 12:11; 1 Cor. 9:24-27; Prov. 22:29

Keys to productive Bible Discussions: As much as possible, Bible discussion should flow with the stage you are in the relationship. It may be helpful to focus on any of the following areas:

- What you can do to have a beautiful future
- Opportunities to explore
- Etc.

Next Meeting

Date | Time, Location

COURTSHIP CONVERSATIONS

Date: Time: Location:

Agenda – Spirituality and Service Issues

1. Spiritual life and commitments to God
   a. Christian experiences
2. Denominational affiliation before marriage
   a. Perspectives
   b. Any concerns?
3. Denominational affiliation after marriage
   a. Where?
   b. Why?
4. Serving God
   a. What are the areas you have been involved in the service of God?
   b. In what ways can you serve God together in the future?
5. Mentors
   a. Who are your mentors before marriage?
   b. Who would be your mentor after marriage?
   c. Will you be okay for your mentor to be mentoring both of you after marriage?

Submissions from Intending Groom

Submissions from Intending Bride

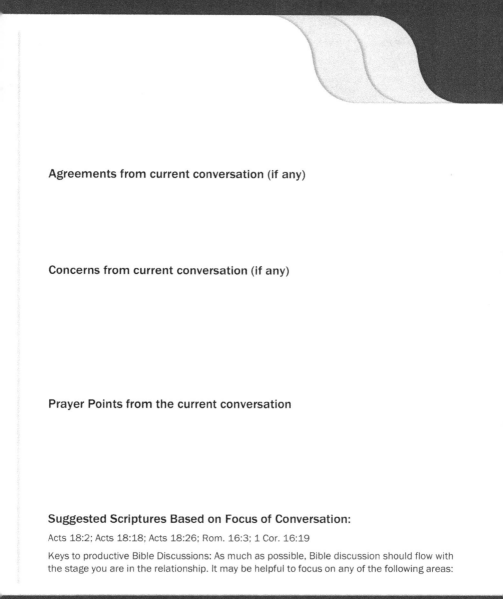

Agreements from current conversation (if any)

Concerns from current conversation (if any)

Prayer Points from the current conversation

Suggested Scriptures Based on Focus of Conversation:

Acts 18:2; Acts 18:18; Acts 18:26; Rom. 16:3; 1 Cor. 16:19

Keys to productive Bible Discussions: As much as possible, Bible discussion should flow with the stage you are in the relationship. It may be helpful to focus on any of the following areas:

- How do you plan to serve God with your marriage?
- Etc.

Next Meeting

Date | Time, Location

COURTSHIP CONVERSATIONS

Date: Time: Location:

Agenda – Casual and domestic issues

1. Dressing styles
   a. Discuss your preferred dressing styles
   b. Discuss your dislikes too

2. What you love to see in the home
   a. List all items
   b. It does not mean you are going to get everything at once. Such conversations makes you to know each other more.

3. Other domestic Issues
   a. Favorite meals and Eating habits
      - Discuss any allergies that you may have.
      - Discuss any preferences that you may have.

   b. Cooking skills:
      - What foods can you prepare?
      - What meals are you not able to prepare?
      - Based on the above preferences, determine if there are skills you need to learn before your marriage.

   c. Perspectives about eating outside the home
      - It is important to discuss any concerns you may have about this topic

   d. Home Design
      - Please spend some time to discuss how you would like your future home to look like, and start working towards it, prayerfully.

   e. Size
      - Do you like a small, medium, or big house?

   f. Etc.

Submissions from Intending Groom

Submissions from Intending Bride

Agreements from current conversation (if any)

Concerns from current conversation (if any)

Prayer Points from the current conversation

Suggested Scriptures Based on Focus of Conversation:

Phil. 4:5; I Tim. 2:9; 1 Cor. 10:31

Keys to productive Bible Discussions: As much as possible, Bible discussion should flow with the stage you are in the relationship. Focusing on any of the following areas may be helpful:

- Principles of moderation and contentment

Next Meeting

Date | Time, Location

COURTSHIP CONVERSATIONS

Date: Time: Location:

Agenda – Relational Issues

1. Respect and submission in the home
   a. Be real with each other
   b. Focus on what the Bible says and let your decisions be scriptural
   c. Validate perspectives from scriptures
2. Resolution of conflicts
   a. Agree on who will be your go-to person when you need counseling.

Submissions from Intending Groom

Submissions from Intending Bride

Agreements from current conversation (if any)

Concerns from current conversation (if any)

Prayer Points from the current conversation

Suggested Scriptures Based on Focus of Conversation:

1 Cor. 11:3; Ephesians 5: 24-33; Ephesians 5: 22-23; Ephesians 5: 21; 1 Pet.3:7; Prov. 22:6.

Keys to productive Bible Discussions: As much as possible, Bible discussion should flow with the stage you are in the relationship. Focusing on any of the following areas may be helpful:

- God's commands to the husband
- God's commands to the wife
- God's command to every couple

Next Meeting

Date | Time, Location

COURTSHIP CONVERSATIONS

Date: Time: Location:

Agenda – Relating with extended families

1. List their names and relationship with you.
   - You can use this as an opportunity to discuss everything that you did not cover during your discussions about your family background

2. Discuss how often you will like to visit your relations
   - E.g., once in a while, during specific times of the year, when the need arises to visit them, etc.).

3. How often would you like extended family members to be visiting you after marriage?
   - For example, when you have a baby, etc.

4. Talk about any foreseeable financial obligations towards extended family relations
   - E.g., you can agree to help relations as the need arises and as God provides for your family. You do not need to have a hard and fast rule.

5. Discuss if there are family members that you have concerns about so that intending partner can be aware ahead of time.

6. Share your views about any family member permanently staying with you after the wedding.

7. Discuss everything.

Submissions from Intending Groom

Submissions from Intending Bride

Agreements from current conversation (if any)

Concerns from current conversation (if any)

Prayer Points from the current conversation

Suggested Scriptures Based on Focus of Conversation:

1 Tim. 5:8

Keys to productive Bible Discussions: As much as possible, Bible discussion should flow with the stage you are in the relationship. Focusing on any of the following areas may be helpful:

- When to help
- How much help you would be rendering
- Etc.

Next Meeting

Date | Time, Location

COURTSHIP CONVERSATIONS

Date: Time: Location:

Agenda – Time management issues

1. How to manage time between your secular, home and spiritual commitments
   - Plan based on your situations
   - How would you manage your time to meet family, spiritual and career demands
   - Discuss time-management tools and softwares that may be helpful to organize and plan schedules, timelines, projects, and family goals.

Submissions from Intending Groom

Submissions from Intending Bride

Agreements from current conversation (if any)

Concerns from current conversation (if any)

Prayer Points from the current conversation

Suggested Scriptures Based on Focus of Conversation:

SOS 1:5,6

Keys to productive Bible Discussions: As much as possible, Bible discussion should flow with the stage you are in the relationship. Focusing on any of the following areas may be helpful:

- What you need to do so your family does not suffer lack of time and parental inattention
- When to prioritize family above anything else
- How you will organize your time and family affairs to ensure you have enough family time together.
- Etc.

Next Meeting

Date | Time, Location

COURTSHIP CONVERSATIONS

Date: Time: Location:

Agenda – Sexuality Issues

1. Family Planning
   a. Number of children
   b. When to start having babies
   c. Family planning options
   d. Other sex-related questions
   e. You must discuss any medical issues that you may have during courtship. The other person should be aware of it before marriage. A broken courtship is better than a broken marriage.

Submissions from Intending Groom

Submissions from Intending Bride

Agreements from current conversation (if any)

Concerns from current conversation (if any)

Prayer Points from the current conversation

Suggested Scriptures Based on Focus of Conversation:

SOS. 2:7; 2:15; 8:4,7; Heb. 13:4

Keys to productive Bible Discussions: As much as possible, Bible discussion should flow with the stage you are in the relationship. Focusing on any of the following areas may be helpful:

- Purity before and in marriage
- Etc.

Next Meeting

Date | Time, Location

COURTSHIP CONVERSATIONS

Date: Time: Location:

Agenda: - Ceremonial Issues (Planning Your Wedding)

1. Marriage Plans
    a. Fix the date for your wedding
        - Involve your parents in your plans
        - Ensure availability of parents on selected dates
        - Check with your church if they are okay with your dates (if you wish to do a church wedding)

    b. File your marriage with the appropriate government agency in your country.
    c. Pay the dowry (if applicable or whatever is required by the families). Note that dowry payment is illegal in some countries. Hence, be sure you have consulted with the appropriate authorities.
    d. Prioritize prayers on all you have discussed and expecting.
    e. Estimate your financial obligations for the ceremony.
        - Have a good plan in place for transportation of people (where necessary), feeding of guests, and all other logistics about the marriage ceremony, etc.
    f. Decide who would be your Best-man and Best-lady. Spend time to pray together.

Submissions from Intending Groom

Submissions from Intending Bride

Agreements from current conversation (if any)

Concerns from current conversation (if any)

Suggested Scriptures Based on Focus of Conversation:

John 2:1-11; Luke 14:28

Keys to productive Bible Discussions: As much as possible, Bible discussion should flow with the stage you are in the relationship. Focusing on any of the following areas may be helpful:

- Put Jesus Christ first in all things.
- Proper planning to prevent failures.
- Financial management to prevent debts.
- Etc.

Next Meeting

Date | Time, Location

Endnotes

1   Fernando Ferreira Costa and Nicola Conran. 2016. Sickle Cell Anemia: From Basic Science to Clinical Practice.

2   Christopher Hillyer Leslie Silberstein Paul Ness Kenneth Anderson John Roback. 2006. Blood banking and transfusion medicine. Hardcover ISBN: 9780443069819. eBook ISBN: 9780702036255. Imprint: Churchill, Livingstone. Published Date: 18th October 2006.

3   https://www.disabled-world.com/calculators-charts/blood-chart.php

4   https://anabaptistworld.org/marriage-ceremonies-bible/

5   https://www.washingtonpost.com/news/acts-of-faith/wp/2016/04/08/the-catholic-church-didnt-even-consider-marriage-a-sacrament-for-centuries/

6   https://en.wikipedia.org/wiki/Marriage_in_the_Catholic_Church#Sacramental_development